A Step BEYOND

Multimedia Activities for Learning American History

Muriel Miller Branch

Earlene Green Evans

Neal-Schuman Publishers, Inc.

New York   London

Published by Neal-Schuman Publishers, Inc.
100 Varick Street
New York, NY 10013

Printed and bound in the United States of America

Library of Congress Cataloging-in-Publication Data

Branch , Muriel Miller .
  A step beyond : multimedia activites for learning American history / by Muriel
M . Branch and Earlene G. Evans.
      p.   cm .
   Includes bibliographical references and index .
   ISBN 1-55570- 195- 7
   1 . United States -- HistoryStudy and teaching .   2 . United States-
  -History--Study and teaching (Elementary)   I . Evans , Earlene G.
  II . Title .
   E175 . 8 . B73   1995
   973 ' . 071 ' 273--dc20   94-37766
                                                        CIP

Contents

Acknowledgements

The authors wish to express their appreciation to the following people for their contributions, support, and encouragement durin the preparation of this manuscript:

Our families

The teachers and students with whom we worked on numerous lessons and activities, especially at Thompson Middle School

Our colleagues in the Department of Media and Technology of Richmond Public Schools

About the Authors

Muriel Miller Branch has devoted over 25 years to doing what she enjoys most, teaching. In 1991, she received an award for teaching excellence which funded her study of the Polynesian, Gullah, Appalachian, and Zuni cultures. Branch is a member of Pi Lambda Theta National Honor Association, Virginia Educational Media Association, The Virginia Breast Cancer Foundation, and the National Association for the Preservation and Perpetuation of Storytelling. She also serves as a mentor for a teen reporter for the **Good News Herald,** a Local Newspaper. Muriel Miller Branch is the author of *The Water Brought Us: The Story of the Gullah-Speaking People*. She co-authored *Miss Maggie: The Story of Maggie Lena Walker*, and *Hidden Skeletons and Other Funny Stories*. She has had articles published in **American Libraries, Mediagram, Public Education in Virginia, About. . . Time Magazine,** and **School Librarian's Workshop.** Muriel Miller Branch lives in Richmond, VA with her husband Willis, her mother, her two daughters, and a granddaughter.

Earlene Green Evans, a veteran teacher/librarian is a recipient of the Rutherford Memorial and Florence B. Duke Awards for excellence in Library Science and a two-time winner of the Virginia Educational Media Association Photography Award. Evans devotes time and energy to the Phi Lambda Theta Professional Honor Society, Saint Paul's College Alumni Association, and Alpha Kappa Alpha Sorority. She participated in the production of a video, "Multimedia Out Of A Box," sponsored by the Virginia Department of Education. Earlene Evans is also involved in a mentoring writing program for teenagers, The Teen Scene, and extension of **The Good News Herald,** and author of *I Love You, Ugly Old Hag*. She has co-authored *Hidden Skeletons and Other Funny Stories*, a book about humor in education, has written articles for a local newspaper, and an article for **About. . . Time Magazine.** Earlene Green Evans resides in Richmond, VA with her husband and two grown children.

Foreword

One often does not have a chance to truly share successes. This book, however, is the sharing by two established authors of activities involving research and thinking skills that have proven to be successful. Having spent, totally, more than a half century as committed library media specialists and authors, Muriel Miller Branch and Earlene Green Evans bring to *A Step Beyond* a wealth of practical experience. Theory is important, but the ability to implement theory is even more so as those of us in the field can attest. After spending several years on the Board of the American Association of School Librarians, and planning, revising and implementing Information Power, I have tremendous respect for these authors and this major undertaking.

This series is filled with activities which allow students to grow in cognitive and research skills. That growth gives them the tools to apply that knowledge to the standardized tests they will take as they move forward in their educational careers. These activities allow those of us who work with today's students to have a resource on which we can depend. Capable of being expanded to all forms of media, laser disks, computer disks, instructional television, these activities allow students to choose the level of information they desire. The challenge of *A Step Beyond* is, in and of itself, a tremendous motivator. Take it, use it with confidence—the students will be the beneficiaries of your legacy.

Dr. Delores Z. Pretlow,
Director of Media and Technology,
Richmond Public Schools, Richmond, Virginia.
Co-Chair, Visions Committee, AASL.

Introduction

A Step Beyond: Multimedia Activities for Learning American History demonstrates the way in which the library media center and its staff can help teachers and their students to break out of the lockstep learning of the single text, the one assignment for everyone, using limited resources. Its shows how students can practice research skills using a wide variety of reference resources and technologies. It does, in short, help teachers and librarians who use it with students to teach that most sought-after of Information Age skills: Information Literacy.

The tasks or activities are proposed under the many subjects related to each of the four major curriculum units covered: Going West, The Civil War, Native Americans, and Alaska. Each topic has differentiated research and challenge tasks to meet the many ability levels and learning styles of middle school learners. Each task is designed to stimulate creative responses and solutions in specific areas of research. The final set of tasks under each topic provides a way for the abler inquirier to go "a step beyond" the required information on the subject to plan and carry out a major creative project related to it. This may take the form of dramatics or role-playing, public performance for a school or larger community audience, preparing an exhibit, or calling on resources outside the school—and more.

For example: the first subject for research under the unit on Going West is "The Big Purchase" and all the tasks associated with it have to do with varied aspects of President Jefferson's "big deal" with France which added not only Louisiana but a good portion of the continent to the young United States. Among the first five tasks is included an opportunity to set up a crossword puzzle on graph paper, using clues about persons and terms connected with the Louisiana Purchase. After these five tasks come the ones that are "a step beyond": "Choose two groups, one to represent America, the other France. Organize a Louisiana Purchase "Summit" between the two countries to work out the details of the transaction. Each delegation must know how its country would benefit, but the American delegation must use all of its persuasive skills to convince the French to sell. . ." Step Beyond item number two for this topic is to "Videotape the 'Summit' and prepare a news special on it to show the class."

The first task of the next subject under Going West asks students to "Use Boolean logic to search an encyclopedia on CD ROM for information about Jefferson's administration." A step beyond assignment, following some research on the Westward Movement asks each student to "take a position for or against the Westward Movement, and organize a class debate on the issues." These call for action and sharing of one's Work are perfectly geared to the energies, creative impulses and need for recognition of typical middle school students.

The interdisciplinary approach of *A Step Beyond: Multimedia Activities for Learning American History* invites students to experience vicariously the drama of history in ways that encourage synthesis and evaluation of information. Furthermore, it is structured so that it enables students to see the connection between american history and math, science, language arts, art and music, but also to be involved actively in establishing these connections.

The "step beyond" tasks at the end of each set of tasks for a subject allow students to demonstrate the information they have gathered in creative ways. Because we believe that middle school learners enjoy sharing their work with an audience, we have built into each set of tasks the opportunity for them to express themselves through a wide range of media and technologies. Videotaping, debating, conduction demonstrations, interviewing, creative dramatics, mock press conferences and political events, art displays, fashion shows and designing puzzles or games are some of the ways in which students are asked to share information and express opinions they have formed.

While the book has a common theme, each activity may be done independently of the others. Teachers and librarians are not limited to using one activity with an entire class, although that is an option. The greatest successes we have had using these and similar themes and tasks, have been acheived with small groups, teams, and individuals. A distinguishing feature of this book which makes it more interesting to students than other thematic research skills books is that it incorporates more heavily than most the use of different types of technology: laser disc, video, automated card catalog, CD-ROM, on-line data bases and other computer programs.

Because these "steps beyond" have increased the learning enjoyment of children while helping them learn skills they will need for the rest of their lives, we offer them to other librarians and teachers and the students they are guiding through the past and into the future.

PART I

Going West

The Louisiana Purchase: The Big Purchase

Tasks

1. What was the Louisiana Purchase?
2. What states did the United States gain from the purchase of the territory?
3. Gradually, the territory bordering the Gulf of Mexico became a haven for thousands of settlers from the southeast. The new territory became known as_____.
4. A copy of the Louisiana Purchase can be found in the *DICTIONARY OF AMERICAN HISTORY*. Why was it such a good "deal" for America.
5. On graph paper, set up a crossword puzzle using the clues about people and terms related to the Louisiana Purchase.

Clues:
Across

1. He purchased the vast area between the Mississippi River and the Rocky Mountains.
2. He accompanied the leader of the expedition.
3. He was commissioned by President Jefferson to lead the expedition.
4. The ocean that borders the United States on the west.

Down

1. The land was purchased from this country.
2. _____Purchase was our country's most important business transaction.

A Step Beyond

1. Choose two groups, one to represent America and the other, France. Organize a "Louisiana Purchase Summit" between the two countries. Work out the details of the transaction. Each delegation must know how its country would benefit, but the American delegation must use all of its persuasive skills to convince the French to sell Louisiana to them.
2. Videotape the "Summit" and prepare a News Special on it to show to the class.

The Louisiana Purchase: Vast Territory

Tasks

Use Boolean logic to search an encyclopedia on CD ROM for information about Thomas Jefferson's administration.

1. During which of President Jefferson's terms in office was the Louisiana Purchase made?
2. Read the information on the computer disk about Thomas Jefferson's presidency.
3. Study the list of subjects in the WORLD BOOK ENCYCLOPEDIA RESEARCH GUIDE about the Westward Movement. Is the subject of the Lewis and Clark Expedition included in the list? How is it listed?

A Step Beyond

1. From what country was the Louisiana Territory purchased? Explain why the country was willing to sell this vast area of land to the United States.
2. Find an article about the Lewis and Clark Expedition in the *WORLD BOOK ENCYCLOPEDIA on* CD ROM.
3. From the information you read, take a position for or against the westward movement, and organize a class debate on the issues.

The Louisiana Purchase: New Territory

Tasks

Use the laser software for "Understanding Our World," *POWERS OF THE PRESIDENT.* Go to Chapter 37 and scan the visual frames listed to the map of the westward expansion.

1. Study the early 1800's map in Chapter 37 and compare it with a current map of the United States.
2. Draw a map of the United States and color in the states which would now be a part of what was the Louisiana Territory.

A Step Beyond

1. Chapter 13, "Understanding Our World," for the laser disk is, "The President and the Media." As the Presidential Press Secretary, prepare Thomas Jefferson for a televised press conference on the success of the Lewis and Clark Expedition. Stage an actual press conference.
2. As a reporter covering the press conference, ask the President questions about the expedition.
3. Use a word processing program to compose and print a message that President Jefferson might have delivered to the country explaining the Lewis and Clark expedition.
4. Write a magazine article about the Lewis and Clark Expedition and design a cover for the magazine.

The Lewis And Clark Expedition: American Explorers

Meriwether Lewis and William Clark were famous American explorers. President Thomas Jefferson instructed them to find a land-water route to the Pacific Ocean. He told them to go up the Missouri River, cross the Continental Divide, and down the Columbia River to its mouth. He further instructed them to gather and record information on geography, mineral resources, Indian tribal organizations and languages, and animal and plant life.

Tasks

1. You have been given the same instructions as Lewis and Clark. Look at a map of the United States. Choose the place where you would begin your expedition. What is there about the place you have chosen that makes it a good place to begin?
2. Use an atlas to locate the Missouri River, The Continental Divide, and the Columbia River. How was each important to the expedition?
3. Write a travel log of the expedition giving the following details:
    A. The state(s) through which you had to travel
    B. The terrain
    C. The climate
    D. The Indian tribes that lived there
4. Which of the following, the terrain, the climate, or the Indians presented the greatest challenge? Why?

A Step Beyond

1. Make a visual comparing the United States as it looked before the expedition and after the Louisiana Purchase.
2. Write President Jefferson a letter reporting the progress of the expedition.

The Lewis And Clark Expedition: Biographies

A biographical dictionary contains very short biographies of well known people. Each entry gives only the most important facts about the person's life. Most biographical sources are arranged in alphabetical order.

Tasks

1. Use a biographical reference book to answer the questions below:
   A. When was Meriwether Lewis born?
   B. Where was he born?
   C. What kind of work did Meriwether Lewis do before he became an explorer?
   D. What influenced him to become an explorer?
2. Write the title of the biographical reference you used.

_____

3. Why was the Lewis and Clark exploration of the west so important to the growth of the United States?
4. Using various biographical sources, gather information about other persons involved with the Lewis and Clark expedition.
   A. Thomas Jefferson
   B. Sajagawea
   C. Toussaint Charbonneau
   D. York (a slave)

A Step Beyond

1. Compare the personalities, skills, and perspective of each of the persons listed in question 4.
2. Define resumé. Write a resume for one of the persons involved in the expedition who is applying for a job with an advertising firm to promote the westward movement.

The Lewis And Clark Expedition: Lewis And Clark Stayed Home 1 (computer game)

Tasks

Use the MECC computer program, "Lewis and Clark Stayed Home" to answer the questions below.

1. Give three reasons for the Lewis and Clark expedition.
2. The computer program cites the expedition party's first stop. Make careful note of this stop, including the name of the area.

A Step Beyond

Select the "New Game" from the menu of LEWIS AND CLARK STAYED HOME. Try getting through the Wilderness Maze by making decisions that an explorer would make.

The Lewis And Clark Expedition Lewis And Clark Stayed Home 2 (computer game)

Tasks

1. Go through the first program on the computer disk, *LEWIS AND CLARK STAYED HOME*. Make selections as requested.
2. Why were Lewis and Clark unable to make the expedition as planned?
3. Did you accept the invitation to take Lewis and Clark's place on the expedition? Why or why not?

A Step Beyond

1. Considering the circumstances of the exploration, make a list of equipment and supplies you would need. Return to the game on the computer disk. Compare the list with yours.
2. Suppose you were leading a similar expedition and could only take one small bag with you. Fill one bag with items which you would have packed in 1804. Fill a second bag with items which you would pack today.
3. Show the class examples of items in each bag and explain their importance to the particular time period.

The Lewis And Clark Expedition: Into The Unknown

Tasks

1. What time of year did Lewis and Clark begin their expedition?
2. What special skills did they need to survive the journey?
3. Draw a map showing the route of the expedition going and returning. Explain why some members of the expedition chose a different route on their return.
4. Keep a daily journal of your travel experiences as Lewis and Clark did. Using your journal to recall the experiences, write a short narrative on what you could have done differently to improve relationships with the Native Americans.

A Step Beyond

1. You have been assigned to cover the expedition for the Weekly News. Write an article for the paper giving a full account of the expedition.
2. In one page, describe how you would feel exploring an unknown place.

Beyond The Fall Line

Tasks

1. Define fall line. Why did the pioneers move west beyond the fall line?
2. Study a map of the United States the way it looked during the 1670's. Point out the fall line on the map.
3. What races of people migrated from the east coast westward?
4. Use a geographical dictionary and other books to define the words listed below.
   - A. Appalachian Mountains
   - B. Continental Divide
   - C. Fall line
   - D. Mississippi River
   - E. Missouri River
   - F. Pacific Ocean
   - G. Pikes Peake
   - H. Rocky Mountains
   - I. Snake River

A Step Beyond

1. Use the words listed in number 4 to create a Seek and Search puzzle.
2. As a developer, initiate an advertising campaign to attract settlers to this newly explored territory.

Legendary Characters

Tasks

1. Locate in a biographical reference, an individual biography, or a collective biography information about one of the persons listed below:

   A. James Beckwourth
   B. Daniel Boone
   C. Jim Bridger
   D. Paul Bunyan
   E. Kit Carson
   F. Buffalo "Bill" Cody
   G. David Crockett
   H. John Henry
   I. Sam Houston
   J. Nat Love
   K. Bill Pickett
   L. Zebulon Pike
   M. Sacajawea
   N. Ted Smith
   O. Tecumesch
   P. Mark Twain
   Q. Marcus Whitman
   R. Brigham Young

A Step Beyond

1. Write a two-page narrative about the person's life and accomplishments from his point of view.
2. Using a biographical dictionary, gather information to create a board game about the persons listed in task 1.

President Jefferson: The Administration

Tasks

1. Study the MECC program, *THE PRESIDENTS*. Answer the questions about Thomas Jefferson.
   - A. Which state was admitted to the union during Jefferson's administration? What year?
   - B. What historical business transaction took place during Jefferson's administration?
2. Was the Burr Conspiracy mention on the computer disk? If yes, what is your understanding of it?

A Step Beyond

1. Make a flag of the United States as it looked during Jefferson's administration.
2. Make a chronology chart of Thomas Jefferson's life.

President Jefferson: Powers Of The President (computer program)

Tasks

1. Use the laser disk player and its software, *POWERS OF THE PRESIDENT* to view the "Presidents of the United States" in Chapter 42. Scan Chapter 42 to identify the president who sent Lewis and Clark on the expedition.
2. Look at a copy of the United States Constitution to identify the specific powers of the President which allowed Thomas Jefferson to commission the expedition and to purchase the territory.

A Step Beyond

1. Which president commissioned the space exploration in the United States? Point out how each exploration opened new frontiers.
2. How did the space exploration and the westward movement change our way of living? Give specific examples.
3. Compare the preparations for travel made by Lewis and Clark to those of astronauts, Neil Armstrong and Edwin Aldrin.

President Jefferson: Vision's of Expansion (CD-ROM software)

Tasks

Use the software for CD ROM and search for information about Thomas Jefferson's administration.

1. What was considered one of President Jefferson's greatest achievement?
2. Under which of Thomas Jefferson's administration was the Louisiana Purchase made?
3. From what country was the Louisiana Territory purchased? In what year was the purchase made?

A Step Beyond

1. The Louisiana Territory lies between two major land forms. Identify them on a map of the United States. Make a relief map showing them.
2. Which two rivers were a part of the newly acquired territory? What effect did the rivers have on the way goods and services were delivered? Create a before and after chart to show the comparisons.

War Of 1812

Tasks

1. List the events which led to the War of 1812. Describe each event.
2. What countries were involved in the War of 1812? Why were they involved?
3. What were the results of the War of 1812?
4. What was the impact of the War of 1812 on the frontier?

A Step Beyond

1. How would life on the frontier have been different had the War of 1812 not been fought?
2. Write a newspaper headline and lead story for one of the events listed.
    - A. Embargo Act passed by Congress
    - B. Leopard attacks Chesapeake
    - C. James Madison asks Congress to declare war against Great Britain
    - D. Battle of New Orleans
    - E. British burn Washington, D. C.
    - F. British ships attack Fort McHenry
    - G. The Treaty of Ghent signed

Inside A Treaty

Task

What is a treaty? Find a copy of a treaty and read it. How was it agreed on?
What were the provisions of this particular treaty? Was this treaty broken?
If so, what were the consequences?

A Step Beyond

Match each ordinance or treaty below with its provision or agreement.
Write the correct letter beside the answer.

   A. Ordinance of 1785
   B. Northwest Ordinance of 1787
   C. Pinkney"s Treaty of 1785
   D. Treaty of Greenville
       Provided for surveys of the Northwest Territory townships 6 miles
       square
    __Set up government for the new area
    __Opened Ohio lands and established definite boundaries between
       Indian lands and those opened to settlement.
    __Settled a conflict with Spain in the Southwest

Inside A Treaty: Classification

Tasks

1. How are treaties classified? Write your understanding of each class.
2. What language were treaties written in before the 1700's?
3. Find biographical information about Peter Minuit. What is the relation-ship between Minuit, a treaty, and Wall Street?

A Step Beyond

1. Think of a disagreement you had with someone. Write a treaty to settle the disagreement. How would your treaty be classified?
2. Get a Latin dictionary and try translating your treaty to Latin.

Westward Bound

Tasks

Use various books and reference sources to answer the questions below:

1. What motivated the Forty-Niners to go west?
2. Describe "the cattle kingdom" on the Great Plains.
3. How long did the westward expansion last and what was the ultimate goal?

A Step Beyond

1. Use the *Dictionary of American History* to do further reading about the westward movement. As you read, make a list of every method of transportation used by the explorers and pioneers. Use the list to make a transportation time line.
2. How have the different modes of transportation affected our lives today?
3. During the westward expansion, important changes in transportation occurred. What were some of these changes and how did they influence the economy of the New Nation?
4. Set up a transportation exhibit in your classroom showing the evolution of transportation in America.

Traveling By Wagon Train

Tasks

1. How did the prairie schooner get its name?
2. How was the scout master helpful to the pioneers who rode the wagon train?
3. Make a list of scout masters who became famous.

A Step Beyond

1. Select one of the famous scout leaders from task number 3.
2. Use a biographical dictionary, the *WORLD BIOGRAPHY* or an encyclopedia to gather information about the scout leader you chose.
3. Use word processing software to type and print your report.

Problems Of The Frontier

Tasks

1. The frontier people faced problems with land, government, and Indians. As a leader on the frontier, how would you have solved some of these problems?
2. What were some of the consequences for the Indians and the settlers when treaties were broken? Give some specific examples.

A Step Beyond

Introduce to the House of Representatives a bill to address one of the problems faced by the settlers.

The Erie Canal: Why It Was Built

Tasks

Using *COMPTON'S MULTIMEDIA ENCYCLOPEDIA on CD ROM* or another encyclopedia on CD ROM, find information on CANALS.

1. What is a canal?
2. What were some of the economic factors behind the building of canals?
3. How did the Erie Canal get its nickname, "Clinton's Ditch"? Tell what happened to change the attitudes of the people after the canal was built.

A Step Beyond

DeWitt Clinton believed that the Erie Canal could and should be built. Although he was criticized for his position, he presented his plan and campaigned to get it done. Read newspaper and magazine articles about a project in your area which is being criticized. Campaign to "sell" the idea to your state legislature as DeWitt Clinton did.

The Erie Canal: Building The Canal

Tasks

1. What was the value of the Erie Canal to the settlers?
2. Trace the route of the Erie Canal from east to west on the map of the United States.
3. What cities and bodies of water does it connect?
4. What are the dimensions of the Erie Canal? What would be the equivalent measurement in metric?
5. Find the name of a canal near you. Write and illustrate a report about the canal.

A Step Beyond

1. Compare the reasons for constructing the Erie Canal with those of constructing the Panama Canal.
2. Compare DeWitt Clinton with a similar personality of your choice.
3. Make a model of a canal.

Native Americans: Dispelling Myths

In the past, many books, movies, and television programs stereotyped Native Americans.

Tasks

1. Define stereotype. Look at an old western movie, and find examples of how Native Americans were stereotyped.
2. Use various materials to locate information about the following Native American tribes/nations to dispel the stereotypes you identified in the movie.
    - A. Apache
    - B. Cherokee
    - C. Cheyenne
    - D. Crow
    - E. Dakota (Sioux)
    - F. Navaho
    - G. Omaha
    - H. Pueblo
3. Prepare a series of three articles for your local newspaper on the contributions of Native Americans which would help to erase the negative attitudes about them. Include pictures in your articles. This is not an opinion piece.

A Step Beyond

1. Divide the class into two groups for a "Speak Out" forum that will allow Native Americans and Pioneers to express their opposing views concerning who should own the land.
2. Write a letter of protest to the President about the treatment of Native Americans. Support your argument/protest with facts from your research.

Native Americans: Myths and Legends

Tasks

1. Native Americans have a rich oral tradition. Find books about Indian legends and myths in the library.
2. Read several Native American myths and legends and compare them to stories from your culture (African American, European, Asian, Hispanic, Jewish).

A Step Beyond

1. Tell or dramatize a Native American folktale to the class.
2. What did you learn about Native American culture and beliefs from the myths and legends you read.
3. Give examples of how Native Americans explained scientific phenomena in their myths.
4. Coyote and Brer Rabbit are tricksters in Native American and African American folk tales. Write a conversation between the two in which they share ways that they have outsmarted other animals.

Native Americans: Folklore

Tasks

Find the best definition for the following words. Write the definition and a clue for each word. If you have a crossword computer program available, use it to construct a crossword puzzle. If you don't have one, use graph paper.

custom
folklore
folktale
tradition
lore
griot
imitation
religion
authentic
ceremony

A Step Beyond

1. Many Native American folk tales attempted to explain things which occurred in nature for which they had no answers. These stories are often referred to as "Why Stories." Locate a Native American folk tale in the card catalog. Read the "Why Stories." What was each story trying to explain?
2. Masks are an important part of Native American ceremonies. Who wears them and for what occasions? Draw some of the most popular Native American masks and tell what tribes they represent.
3. Prepare a mask-making demonstration for the class.

Americans: Legendary Characters

People like Paul Bunyan, John Henry , Pecos Bill, Buffalo Bill Cody, Kit Carson, and David Crockett were legendary heroes.

Tasks

1. Paul Bunyan and John Henry showed incredible strength, and they each became noted for their manual labor. Write an article for Outdoorsman Magazine describing some of their extraordinary feats.
2. Describe the relationship that Buffalo Bill Cody, Kit Carson and David Crockett had with the Native Americans (Indians).
   A. What tribes did they encounter?
   B. How did the Native Americans help them?

A Step Beyond

Write an original legend about one of the folk heroes of the west.

A Poetic Experience

Tasks

1. Use the subject index to *GRANGER'S INDEX TO POETRY* to find a poem about each of the subjects listed below:
   - A. Explorers and Exploring
   - B. Rocky Mountains
   - C. Pioneers
   - D. Indians, American
2. List the author (if given) and title of at least one poem under each subject which most closely relates to your study of the westward movement.
3. Use the "Title and First Line" index to find the symbols for the books in which the poems appear. Write all of the symbols. Example: All along the rail. In Texas Grass Quincy Troupe. PoBA (PoBA is the symbol used for this poetry anthology).
4. Find PoBA in the "Key to Symbols" in the front of *GRANGER'S INDEX TO POETRY*. Write the title of the book in which it appears.
5. Using an on-line search station, do a title search to find the book.

A Step Beyond

1. If you had been a poet during pioneer days, what kinds of things would you have written about?
2. Working cooperatively with a small group, write poems about pioneer life for a book of poetry. Plan a poetry reading and invite other students.

Historical Fiction: *A Circle Unbroken*
by Sollace Hotze

Tasks

1. Use the card catalog to find the book, *A CIRCLE UNBROKEN* by Sollace Hotze.
2. Read the summary or annotation of the story.
3. Read the book and make notes of historical details which are true to the period.
4. Why is the book classified as a historical novel?
5. Find titles of other books about Indian family life or pioneer family life. Which subjects did you search?

A Step Beyond

1. Locate other historical fiction books in the card catalog. Make an annotated bibliography of the books you find.
2. Create a book cover and "blurb" for one of the historical fiction books from the bibliography.

A Circle Unbroken: Living With The Indians

Tasks

1. Read the book, *A CIRCLE UNBROKEN* by Sollace Hotze. Write answers to the questions below.
    - A. Who is the main character in the story?
    - B. How did Rachel lose her white identity?
    - C. What problems did Rachel encounter with her white family?
2. How did each member of Rachel's family feel toward her?

A Step Beyond

1. Compare an average day in Rachel's white family's home to her Indian family's tepee. How were the families alike? How did they differ?

A Circle Unbroken: Rachel's Dilemma

Tasks

1. In the historical novel by Sollace Hotze, *A CIRCLE UNBROKEN*, what made Rachel's natural father decide to return her to the Sioux?
2. If you do not agree with his decision, write a letter persuading him to change his mind.

A Step Beyond

1. The story, *A CIRCLE UNBROKEN*, takes place in 1838. What important historical events occurred between 1834 and 1848?
2. Write a short historical fiction story based on one of the events.

Natural Forces: Explorer's Traveling Problems

Tasks

1. Which heavenly bodies did the explorers depend upon to guide their travels? Tell how each may have been used.
2. What would be the advantage of traveling during the day? What would be the advantage of traveling at night? Make a chart showing the comparisons.
3. What weather conditions might have delayed their rate of travel in each of the seasons?

A Step Beyond

1. Make a mural of the night sky for all four seasons. Label the constellations that you can see with the naked eye.
2. Construct a simple compass. Test it out of doors for accuracy.
3. Make a list of other means of finding directions. Explain how each is helpful.

The Pioneers: Social Activities

Tasks

1. Read about the social activities of the pioneers. Write answers to the following questions:
    A. Give two examples showing how the pioneers combined work and play.
    B. Describe a typical colonial wedding celebration.
    C. How was music provided for pioneer activities?
2. What games did the pioneer children play that are still played today?

A Step Beyond

1. Get a book about square dancing from your library. Read about the calls and commands used in square dancing.
2. Obtain a square dance record from your library. Listen to the "Red River Valley", the "Virginia Reel" or a square dance of your choice. Teach the dance to a small group.
3. Write and illustrate the directions for playing one of the games played by pioneer children. Demonstrate it for the class.

PART II

The Civil War

Abolitionist Movement

Introduction

The American Civil War was one of the most tragic wars this country has ever engaged in. It divided the country, families, and friends. In this unit we will explore the causes, effects, and important personalities of the period. One group of people, the abolitionists, abhorred slavery and worked hard to abolish it.

Tasks

1. Discuss the significance of the abolitionist movement in the United States. Who were the key players? Why were they so important to the movement?
2. Make a list of at least twenty abolitionists (men, women, African American, Caucasian, Indian, Southerners, Northerners, rich and poor.) Explain who they were and what they contributed to the movement.

A Step Beyond

Using your research, compile a biographical dictionary of abolitionists to be published by Thompson Press. Remember that the biographies must be brief and concise.

African American Soldiers

One group of military heroes has been overlooked in many history books—the African American soldier. The African American soldier fought valiantly and loyally on both sides — the Confederate and the Union.

Tasks

1. Find information about the role of the African American soldier in the Civil War. Take notes.
2. Choose one significant battle fought by African Americans to highlight for the class. Try to find details that are not well known. (Describe the place, dress, weapons, training, leaders, conditions under which they fought, and the outcome of the battle.)

A Step Beyond

1. Draw a map depicting where the battle took place. Pretend you were there and describe the battle to the class.
2. Write a poem or song about your adventures as a "Colored" soldier in either the Union or Confederate army. Present it to the class.

Battles

Tasks

Numerous Civil War battles were fought in the north and south. Some of the most noted were Fort Sumter, First Bull Run (Manassas) Antitham, Gettysburg, Vicksburg, and Chancellorsville.

Describe the importance of each of the battles listed above to the Union and the Confederates.

A Step Beyond

Enlarge a drawing of one of the battles and be prepared to brief the class on what happened.

Causes And Effects of the War

Tasks

1. Read about the causes and effects of the Civil War. Explain why they are considered major. Which cause would you consider the most significant?
2. Explain the causes and effects from a northerner's and a southerner's point of view.

A Step Beyond

From your research, prepare a ten-minute television documentary on the causes and effects of the Civil War. Cover key people, economic, social, political, and ideological reasons. Use charts, graphs, interviews, and excerpts from debates, to enhance your documentary).

Civil War Leaders

Introduction

Some of the most noted Civil War leaders were: John Fremont, Ambrose E. Burnside, Thomas J. "Stonewall" Jackson, George B. McClellan, Robert E. Lee, J. E. B. Stuart, J. S. Mosby, Abner Doubleday, George Custer, P. J. T. Beauregard, and Jefferson Davis.

Tasks

1. Identify all of the leaders listed above.
2. Give details about the battles they led and the outcome of the battles.
3. Discuss the advantages and disadvantages faced by leaders on both sides.

A Step Beyond

Choose one leader. Follow his career from the beginning to the end of the Civil War. Write a brief biography of his military life.

On The Battlefield

Tasks

1. Call the tourist information center in your area and request information about a Civil War battlefield site.
2. If you live in a state outside of the area where the Civil war was fought, choose a battle from the encyclopedia index to research. Write the tourist bureau of the state in which the battle was fought. Request information. You may also want to write National Park Service for information.
3. Interview local historians or National Park Service employees for details and historical facts. What impact did the battle have on the outcome of the Civil War?

A Step Beyond

1. Prepare a video on the battle, using music, maps, charts, and dramatization.
2. Prepare a video of your interview with the local historian or National Park Service employee.

Campaigns and Battles

Tasks

1. Look in the encyclopedia index to find Civil War-Military Campaigns and Battles. Write the volume and page number for each of the following battles:

   Bull Run _____

   New Mexico _____

   Fort Sumter _____

   Chattanooga _____

2. In a paragraph, describe the battles listed above. Include where they were fought, the military leader or leaders of each, and who won.

A Step Beyond

1. On a map of the United States, label the site of at least ten major battles or campaigns of the Civil War.

2. Write and illustrate a picture book for the 7-9 year old of a battle of your choice.

Bearing Arms: Weapons of the War

Tasks

1. List some of the weapons which were used in the Civil War. What special skills may have been needed to use each weapon?
2. How did the invention of the rifle change the fighting tactics?
3. Which side, Union or Confederate, had the most advanced weapons? Why? Support your answer with facts gathered from books, encyclopedias, laser discs, CD ROM, filmstrips, and video tapes.

A Step Beyond

1. Choose one weapon from the list you developed. Pretend you are a salesperson for the manufacturer. Prepare a sales brochure, giving the perspective buyer all of the facts he or she needs to make an intelligent decision. Include such things as special features, price, and operation.
2. Visit the historical society in your area to see if it has copies of newspaper advertisements of various weapons used in the Civil War. Write a newspaper ad for the weapon you have chosen.

Emancipation Proclamation

Tasks

1. The Emancipation Proclamation has been hailed as the document which freed the slaves. Was it? Read a copy of the Emancipation Proclamation and decide for yourself if its purpose was to free slaves. Support your decision with facts.
2. Prepare a rebuttal for the statement, "The Emancipation Proclamation freed the Negro slaves."

A Step Beyond

Write a story for the newspaper, **The Richmond Bugle**, highlighting the events on the day of the Emancipation Proclamation. Cover the reactions of slaves, slave owners, politicians, military leaders, and abolitionists.

Proclaiming Freedom

Tasks

1. Read background information about the Emancipation Proclamation on the encyclopedia on CD ROM. Print the article or take notes.
2. How did the Emancipation Proclamation affect the slaves in the Confederate states?
3. What slave states were not affected by the Emancipation Proclamation?
4. Use the card catalog or the search terminals to find a book about the Constitution of the United States. Which amendment directly affected slavery and how? Explain specific provisions or language in the amendment that had a direct bearing on slavery.

A Step Beyond

1. Draw an outline map of the United States as it looked in 1863.
2. Select a color of your choice to fill in the states or territories that *were* affected by the Emancipation Proclamation.
3. Use a different color to fill in the slave states that *were not* affected by the Emancipation Proclamation.

Suit Up!: Civil War Uniforms

Tasks

1. Study the careers of several military leaders of the Civil War. Which leader would you have preferred to serve under? Give specific reasons for your choice. Use statistics such as wins, loses, fatalities, etc. to support your choice.

A Step Beyond

1. Locate books on clothing or military uniforms worn by Union and Confederate soldiers.
2. Suit Up! Dress up as the Civil War leader you chose. Be as authentic as possible. Give a ten minute speech about your military career.

Newspapers: The Liberator and The North Star

Introduction

Newspapers were crucial to getting information to the citizenry during the before and during the Civil War. Two of the most influential newspapers for the abolitionists were **The Liberator** and **The North Star.**

Tasks

1. Find out who published each of these newspapers. Why were they started?
2. Do you see any importance in the names of the two newspapers? Why do you think they were so named?
3. Give some background information about each editor/publisher.

A Step Beyond

Write a feature article about the Fugitive Slave Laws for **The Liberator** and **The North Star.** (Think about the slant that each might have).

Military Terms: What's In A Name ?

Tasks

1. Use the dictionary or the dictionary feature of CD ROM to find the meaning of the following military terms:
   ammunition
   artillery flank
   infantry ironclad
   ordnance
   regiment
   rifling
   siege
   musket
   theater
   torpedoes
2. Write or print the definition on the computer if the software enables you to do so.

A Step Beyond

1. Using the terms and definitions, design a set of study prints.
2. Using computer software such as ClarisWorks, PageMaker, or Word-Perfect, design a picture dictionary of the military terms listed in task number one. You may add other terms if they relate to the Civil War.
3. If you have access to multimedia (HyperCard), prepare a computer "stack" of each term. Pull images from photographs, drawings, video clips, and CD ROM for a multimedia presentation.

Indentured Servants

Task

Answer the questions below:

1. Who were the indentured servants?
2. Where did most of them come from?
3. Why were they needed in America?
4. What were the conditions under which they came?

A Step Beyond

1. Write a letter to your parents who still live in your home country. Tell them about your experiences and treatment as an indentured servant in America.
2. Contrast the life of an indentured servant with that of a Negro slave.

Sherman's March

Tasks

1. One of the most noted events in Civil War history was Sherman's March to the sea. What was it? Where did it take place?
2. Why was the march so important?
3. What kind of impact did it have on the people who lived in the area?

A Step Beyond

Pretend you are a reporter (on location) covering Sherman's March. Tell your listening or reading audience what you see.

Undercover: Wartime Spies

Introduction

Espionage is essential to collecting classified information about the enemy. The Van Lew Mansion in Richmond, Virginia was reported to be a "spy" center and a "station" on the Underground Railroad.

Tasks

1. Locate information on several of the most noted Civil War spies. Discuss what they did, and why the role they played was so important.
2. Locate information about the Van Lews of Richmond. Were they spies or just sympathizers? Support your answer with facts. Give a brief biographical sketch of the Van Lews.

A Step Beyond

Sometimes spy stories are exaggerated and become legends. Write a legend or folktale about the Van Lews.

Speaking In Codes: The Underground Railroad

Tasks

1. View the video, RACE TO FREEDOM. Look and listen carefully for particular code words used in the video.
2. Write your own definition of each word and provide a brief description of what was happening in the story at the time.

A Step Beyond

1. In any secret mission, codes are very important. Using the code words learned from the video, write a letter to a friend in Canada telling him or her of your planned escape from slavery.
2. Develop your own code words for the Underground Railroad which might be different from those used in the video. What are some words that might be appropriate today?
3. Draw a treasure map for slaves to use along an imaginary Underground Railroad route. Use code words from the film or the ones you created for clues. The treasure is FREEDOM!

How They Got Over: Slave Escapes

Tasks

1. Research four of the most well-known slave escapes in U. S. History.
   William and Ellen Craft
   Henry "Box" Brown
   Sojourner Truth
   Harriet Tubman
2. Take notes on the forms of transportation or method of escape that each used. In your opinion, which escape was the most daring? Why?

A Step Beyond

From the information you gathered, prepare a video on "Great Slave Escapes".

Getting There: Wartime Travel

Tasks

1. List all the means of travel during the Civil War. Give specific examples of changes in transportation which occurred during that period.
2. Compare the railroad systems in the north and south. Which side had the more advanced railroads? How do you think it effected the outcome of the Civil War?
3. Prepare a chronological chart showing the advancement of railroads in the United States.

A Step Beyond

1. On a map of the United States, draw and label the railroad systems during the Civil War.
2. Visit a railroad museum near you. Take note of the special features of trains used during the Civil War. Build a model of one of those trains to scale.

Slaves: Daily Treatment

Tasks

1. How slaves were treated is still being debated by historians today. You be the judge. Locate as much information as you can, from as many sources as you can, about the treatment of Negro slaves in America.
2. Make certain that you have information on both sides of the issue or from two perspectives.
3. Take notes.

A Step Beyond

1. Compare a slave's account of the way he was treated with a slave owner's account.
2. Write a short skit based on a slave narrative to dramatize for the class.

Uncle Tom's Cabin: **Writing A Book Report**

Introduction

When Harriet Beecher Stowe wrote *Uncle Tom's Cabin*, she probably did not realize it would draw so much attention to the evils of slavery.

Tasks

1. Summarize the effects of this book upon the country at this time?
2. Why do you think *Uncle Tom's Cabin* had such a great impact?
3. Give specific examples of stereotyping in *Uncle Tom's Cabin*.

A Step Beyond

Write two book reviews for *Uncle Tom's Cabin*. Write one from a pro-slavery stance and one from an antislavery stance.

Stirring Words: Slave Narratives

Tasks

1. On what date did the first installment of Harriet Beecher Stowe's *Uncle Tom's Cabin* appear? List some other events which occurred during the decade, 1850-1860.

2. In your opinion, what factors may have caused so much debate over a fictional account of slavery.

3. Search the on-line card catalog for books of slave narratives. Read two of them.
   Craft. *Running A Thousand Miles For Freedom*
   Blockson. *The Underground Railroad*
   Bontemps. *Great Slave Narratives*
   Hensen. *Out Of This Place*
   Still. *The Underground Railroad*

A Step Beyond

Based on the slave narratives you read, cite four or five scenes in *Uncle Tom's Cabin* which could have happened in real life. Cite four or five examples of things that could not have happened.

Freedmen

Tasks

1. Who was a freedman?
2. Define manumission.
3. Consult books on slavery and reference books on African American history for the names of some freedmen in the north and in the south.
4. Elaborate on some of the ways they became free.

A Step Beyond

In southern cities such as Charleston, South Carolina and Richmond, Virginia and in northern cities such as Philadelphia, Pennsylvania and Boston, Massachusetts, there were many freed slaves. Prepare a poster size chart, comparing one freedman from each of the cities listed above. Pay special attention to where they lived, their socioeconomic status, the work they did, the impact they had on the abolition of slavery, their education, and what they did after the Civil War.

Underground Railroad

Tasks

1. We have all heard of the Underground Railroad, but what we may not know how extensive it was. Find two of the most heavily traveled Underground Railroad routes.
2. What was so significant about these routes? Who were some of the key conductors along these routes? Where did the routes begin and end? Why were these Underground Railroad routes necessary?

A Step Beyond

1. Make a visual (transparency, poster, map) of two of the Underground Railroad routes. Label the states through which they ran and the key stations along the routes.
2. Which route would you have preferred to have taken? Why?

Famous First Facts of The Civil War

Tasks

Use *Famous First Facts* or the *Book Of Facts* to find the answers to the following historical firsts:

1. What was the first state to secceed from the union?
2. When was the first rifle used in the Civil War?
3. When and where did the first attack of the Civil War take place?
4. Who was the first United States president to be assassinated?
5. What was the first battle won by the Union?
6. What northern state issued the first call for black troops in the Civil War?
7. What was the first battle won by the Confederates?
8. What was the first black regiment organized in the north?
9. Who was the first black Colonel to command a black regiment?
10. Who was the first black man to receive the U.S. Medal of Honor?
11. Who was the first person to use land mines in the Civil War?
12. Where was the first capital of the Confederacy located?
13. When was the first attack submarine used?
14. When was the first telegraph used in the Civil War?
15. When did the wartime military draft begin?
16. When was the first manned balloon put into service in the Civil War?
17. When was the bugle call, "Taps" first used?
18. When was the first ambulance-wagon used to transport wounded soldiers?
19. When was the First Battle of Manassas fought?
20. What was the name of the first ironclad ship to be used in battle?

A Step Beyond

Use the answers to Civil War: Famous First Facts and other first facts that you may have found in your research to organize and stage a game show on the order of Jeopardy.

In The Cards: Using The Card Catalog

Tasks

1. Use the sample card to answer the questions below.

The Civil War
973.7 Pratt, Fletcher.
The Civil War; illus. by Lee J. Ames. Garden City Books. 1955.
62p illus
The author has explained and simplified the famous battles of the war and their significance, as well as describing the colorful personalities on both sides.

1 U.S.-History-Civil War I Title

A. The sample card is a_____card.
B. The author is _____.
C. The complete call number for this book is _____.
D. Write the annotation for this book on the lines below.

_____
_____
_____

E. The title of this book is_____.
F. List the subject under which this book is found.

_____

2. Find another book in the card catalog or the on-line catalog by Fletcher Pratt.

A Step Beyond

Locate three books on the Civil War published in the last ten years. Write a review of each book.

Casualties of War: Comparing The Civil War to Recent Wars

Tasks

1. How many lives were lost in the Civil War?
2. How many lives were lost in World War I, World War II, the Korean Conflict and Vietnam War?
3. What is the percentage of lives lost in World War I, the Korean Conflict, and the Vietnam War to those lost in the Civil?

A Step Beyond

1. Rank the battles of the Civil War in ascending order according to the number of casualties.
2. Use a piece of graphing software to plot the number of casualties for each battle.
3. Design a national monument or memorial to the Civil War soldiers who died in service.

Civil War Careers

Tasks

1. Use the index to the *Encyclopedia Of American History* to locate the following
   jobs held by people during the Civil War:
   blacksmiths
   bugle boys
   clerks
   cobblers
   cooks
   factory workers
   farmers
   laundresses
   nurses
   schoolmistresses/schoolmasters
   scouts
   seamstresses
   shipbuilders
   spies
   surgeons
2. View the movie, GLORY and identify jobs performed by the characters in it. Make a list, describe the jobs, and explain the importance of each job to the Civil War. Explain why some of these jobs may not exist today. What technological advances may have made them obsolete.

A Step Beyond

Hold a Civil War Career Fair. Have selected members of your class to portray a character in the film and explain his or her job.

They Said It: Famous Sayings Before and During The War

Tasks

Use *Bartlett's Familiar Quotations* to locate famous sayings of people before and during the Civil War. Some names you might want to consider using are: John Brown, Frederick Douglass, Frances Ellen Watkins Harper, Levi Coffin, William Craft, Ellen Craft, William Still, and Sojourner Truth.

A Step Beyond

Make a small desk calendar of notable quotes, using a different quote for each day.

Flags: Confederate and Union

Tasks

1. Use a book of flags from the 929s to find a picture of two flags that were flown by the south during the Civil War. What were the names of these flags?
2. Study the Confederate flags carefully as you read. Use the computer to write a descriptive meaning of the symbols used on each flag.
3. Use the flag book to see how many state flags bear the stars and bars. Indicate these states on a map of the United States. What part of the country are the states located?
4. Use felt, construction paper or other supplies to make copies of the two Confederate flags used during the Civil War.

Clothing: Types of Uniforms

Tasks

1. Use the card catalog or a search station to locate a book about historical costumes.
2. Visit a Civil War or an historical museum in your city or town. Observe the uniforms worn by the Union and Confederate soldiers.
3. Make notes of the kinds of materials that were commonly used in the uniforms.
4. Make a list of other items that were a part of the Civil War soldiers uniforms. What was the purpose of these items?
5. Try to attend a reenactment of Civil War activities in your area. Note the uses of the articles attached to the uniforms.

A Step Beyond

Dress a Union and a Confederate doll using fabric, notions, and other items gathered.

All Dressed Up: Civilian Clothing

Tasks

1. View the video disk, CIVIL WAR. Observe the dress of people other than soldiers.
2. Describe basic dress of the following southern persons:
   - A. ladies (white, rich, poor)
   - B. men (white, rich, poor)
   - C. children (white, rich, poor)
   - D. farmers
   - E. slaves (male, female, children, house, field)
3. Considering the climate, the social and economic conditions, and the natural resources, explain how each group of person's dress was affected.

A Step Beyond

1. Use the bar code scanner or step button on the video disk player to locate frames on the disc which show the dress of persons listed in task number
2. Using the selected images, make an oral presentation to the class describing and explaining each person's dress.

Abraham Lincoln: His Life

Tasks

1. View and study a filmstrip or video on Abraham Lincoln.
2. How did Lincoln's background affect his attitude toward the dispute between the north and the south over slavery?

A Step Beyond

Use the book, *Vital Speeches* to find the speech made by Abraham Lincoln in his second inaugural address. Pull out any statements that showed he did not have ill feelings toward those who opposed his philosophy.

Abraham Lincoln: The Presidency

Tasks

1. Use an encyclopedia or any book containing facts about the presidents. Find the name of the president who was elected one hundred years after Abraham Lincoln was elected.

2. Listen to an audio cassette of Lincoln's "Gettysburg Address." Close your eyes and try to visualize the president making his famous speech.

3. Make a chart comparing/contrasting President Lincoln with the president that you found in task number 1. Include in your chart the following information:
   - A. Name of Presidents
   - B. Education
   - C. Party
   - D. Basic Philosophy
   - E. Term in Office
   - F. Religion
   - G. Profession Before Presidency
   - H. Vice President
   - I. Major Accomplishment While In Office
   - J. Cause of Death

A Step Beyond

Use the book, *Vital Speeches* or a book about Abraham Lincoln to find the "Gettysburg Address." Memorize the speech and dress as Lincoln for a contest to be judged by appointed persons.

Medicine: Treating Diseases

Tasks

1. Use a medical dictionary or the dictionary on CD ROM to define the illnesses or diseases below:
    - A. malaria
    - B. fever
    - C. pneumonia
    - D. rheumatism
    - E. diarrhea
    - F. venereal disease
    - G. combat fatigue
    - H. nostalgia
    - I. measles
    - J. smallpox
    - K. tuberculosis
2. Find out how these diseases or illnesses were treated during the Civil War.
3. Find out how these diseases are treated today.

A Step Beyond

With the help of an adult, assemble common household items that are used to cure illnesses. Ask the adult to explain what each item is used for. Could these items have been effective for treating the sick and wounded soldiers? In what ways?

Medicine: Doctors

Tasks

1. Use the *Occupational Outlook Handbook* to read about the professions of a doctor and pharmacist.
2. Interview a doctor and pharmacists on video camera to find out how much training is required to get a MD or a degree in Pharmacy.

A Step Beyond

1. From the information you obtained in reading about medicine during the Civil War, reconstruct the daily routine of a surgeon during that time.
2. Follow and record by video camera the daily routine of a general practitioner. Share your findings about both doctors with the class.

Filibustering: The Emancipation Proclamation

Tasks

1. Define "filibuster."
2. Define "debate."
3. Compare "filibuster" and "debate."
4. View C SPAN to see how a filibuster is conducted in Congress.

A Step Beyond

1. Take a pole to see how many of your classmates agree or disagree with the Emancipation Proclamation.
2. You, a member of Congress support the southern plantation owners. Prepare a filibuster against the Emancipation Proclamation.
3. Take a poll to see if you won supporters.

PART III

Native Americans

Before Columbus

Tasks

1. View Section A: Prehistory to 1680 on THE AMERICAN HISTORY video disc.
    - A. Where is the Bering Strait?
    - B. What is the migration theory associated with it?
    - C. How does the map in frame A1 differ from the one in A2?
2. From the video disc, identify the Native American cultures in the Mesoamerica period. Tell what each civilization left behind to show their culture.
3. Compare the Native Americans of the Mesoamerica period with the ancient Phoenicians.

A Step Beyond

View a videocassette on the Mesa Verde. Make a model of the Mesa Verde.

Physical Characteristics

Tasks

1. View a filmstrip or videocassette about several different Native American tribes and study their physical characteristics.
2. Write five facts about the physical characteristics of Native Americans.
3. What common myth were you able to dispel as a result of viewing the filmstrip or videocassette?

A Step Beyond

1. Find pictures of famous Native Americans. If visible, remove the names from the front of the pictures and put them on the back. See how many students can identify the Native Americans from sight.
2. Collect pictures of different Native Americans. Use the pictures to make a collage. Display the collage in the classroom or hall.

Black Indians

Tasks

1. Locate a copy of William Katz's *Black Indians*. Read it.
2. Why do you think Katz gave his book the subtitle, *A Hidden Heritage*? Give some examples.
3. Identify the following Black Indians by tribe: Crispus Attucks, Paul Cuffee, Langston Hughes, Edmonia "Wildfire" Lewis and Bill Pickett.
4. Find interesting facts about each of the Native Americans given above.

A Step Beyond

Use the facts you gathered in task number four to create a game called, "This is Your Life: A Game of Identification".

Genealogy

Tasks

1. Trace your family's roots back to a particular state in the United States.
2. Locate that state on a map of the United States and list the major Native American tribes in it.

A Step Beyond

1. Use word processing software to compose a narrative explaining how your family might have been helped by Native Americans in the area in which they settled.
2. Draw a family tree to show your Native American roots, if any.

Who Was Who?

Tasks

1 Use the CD ROM or a biographical source to find basic information about the Native Americans below.
   - A. Cornplanter
   - B. Deloria Vine, Jr.
   - C. Marie Dorion
   - D. Alexander McGillivray
   - E. Wilma Mankiller
   - F. Ely Samuel Parker
   - G. King Philip
   - H. Susan LaFlesche Picotte
   - I. John Ross
   - J. Washakie
   - K. Wovoka

2. Use a word processing program to record the information about the Native Americans in task number one. Include their birth or death date, the origin of their name and their contributions to the United States.

3. From the list that you have researched, select one person to interview. Make a list of questions you would ask that person relative to his/her profession or cause.

A Step Beyond

Ask your librarian for permission to set up in the library a portrait gallery of prominent Native Americans.

Who Is Who?

Tasks

1. Use the *Current Biography* or other current biographical sources to find the address of the Native Americans below. Use a word processing program to write a letter to one of them, supporting or opposing their cause.
   A. Joseph Bruhac
   B. Charles Eastman
   C. Wilma Mankiller
   D. N. Scott Momaday
   E. Maria Tallchief
   F. Deloria Vine, Jr.
2. Find out if there is a Native American living in your area. If so, invite him/her to your class for an informal talk.

A Step Beyond

Organize a "Native American History Week". Over the public address system, give a biographical sketch of a different Native American each day.

Children

Tasks

1. Use the CD ROM or an encyclopedia to find information about Indian children and children of two other ethnic groups. Make a parallel chart showing the differences or similarities of each child.
2. Use a book about names to find an example of a Native American child's name, a Japanese child's name, a Caucasian child's name and an African American child's name. Write the meaning of each name. How does the name relate to the child's culture?

A Step Beyond

Each member of the class will find the meaning of his/her name. Write the meaning of the name on a decorated disc to be worn around the neck. Refer to your classmate by his alternate name for a day.

Bearing Gifts

Tasks

1. You want to give your Native American playmate a gift. Make him a gift that will be very special.
2. Take a picture of the gift you made and tell why you made it.

A Step Beyond

Use the PRINT SHOP software or another computer graphic program to make invitations for the baby in task #1 whose family would be having a naming ceremony. Explain the naming ceremony.

Boundaries: Regions Where Each Tribe Lived

Tasks

1. On a map of the United States, write the major Native tribes in the region where they live.
2. In which regions of the United States are the largest tribes concentrated?
3. Discuss the living conditions and traditions of the Native Americans of each region.

A Step Beyond

Divide the class into two groups, representing Native American teens from two different regions. Plan "A Day in the life of…" activity for each tribe.

What's Cooking?

Tasks

1. Use the on-line search station or the card catalog to find books about Native Americans.
2. How did the Native Americans preserve their food?
3. What vegetables were grown by different Native Americans?
4. What wild plants were used for food?
5. What animals were used for food?
6. Which tribe was noted for making "piki?" Describe the procedure of making piki to the class.

A Step Beyond

1. What Native American methods of preserving food do we use today? Bring to class a sample of food preserved by this method.
2. Most Native Americans ate breakfast ONLY after hunting for it. List the steps you would take if you had to hunt for your breakfast tomorrow morning.
3. Bring to class a sample of foods given to us by Native Americans that we still eat today. Have a tasting party.

Corn: Ears A Plenty

Tasks

1. Use the dictionary or the dictionary on CD ROM to define "maize". How does maize relate to corn?
2. Why was corn so important to the Native Americans?
3. Get some dried corn from home, a grocery store or a seed store and demonstrate to the class how corn is ground.
4. Plant some of the corn seeds, using the same techniques used by Native Americans.

A Step Beyond

Plan a "Corn Festival" for the class. Share foods made from corn recipes.

Dressing Up: Regional Cultural Dressing

Tasks

1. Native American dress varied from region to region and culture to culture. Describe the traditional dress of the following tribes:
    - A. Chilcat - Northwest Coast
    - B. Navajo - Southwest
    - C. Chicasaw - Southeast
    - D. Seminole - Southern
    - E. Iroquois - Woodlands
    - F. Cheyenne - Plains
    - G. Inuit - Arctic
2. Use an atlas to find the natural resources used for clothing in the states which comprise each region. List them.

A Step Beyond

1. Make a large model of a map of the United States and label the geographical regions in task number two. Bring in samples of the natural resources if possible and place them in the appropriate regions.
2. Have a fashion show of traditional dress from each geographic region. Include male and female traditional dress. Ask a classmate to narrate the fashion show. Videotape it.

Home Sweet Home: Types Of Housing

Tasks

1. Use the on-line search station or the card catalog to find books about Native Americans.
2. Use the books you found to get information about Native Americans homes.
3. Design a chart showing the name of each Indian tribe you found, the region the tribe lived in and the name of their house.
4. On a map of the United States, draw the types of houses built in each region. Why do you think each tribe chose this type of housing?

A Step Beyond

1. Of the Native American tribes and houses you have studied, choose one that you favor. Construct a diaroma of the Native American village or dwelling.
2. Use necessary materials and supplies to construct for display, models of various Native American houses.

To The Point: Minerals Used For Making Spear Heads

Tasks

1. Which two minerals were most commonly used to make spear points and arrowheads? Why?
2. Use MAC USA software to draw a map of the United States and label where the following types of arrowheads or spear points originated: Sandia point, Clovis point, Folsom point, Inuit ivory point, copper point, bird point, polished stone point, iron arrowheads and spear points.
3. Using an integrated word processing and graphics or paint program, write a description of each arrowhead or spear point, and illustrate it. Make transparencies of each page, and present them in class.

A Step Beyond

Make a bow, using the same procedures that Native Americans used. You may have to substitute some materials. Ask your physical education teacher to teach you how to use it. Ask your physical education teacher to teach you and your classmates how to play archery. Have a contest to see who can come closest to hitting the "bull's eye".

The Big Dogs: Buffalo

Tasks

1. Use the CD ROM or a reference book to find out which Native American tribes found the buffalo to be most useful.
2. Find the names of other members of the buffalo family. Would these animals have been as useful to the Native Americans as the buffalo was? Defend your answer.
3. Outline the method used by Native Americans of hunting and killing buffaloes.
4. What modern name is given to the buffalo?
5. Visit a nearby zoo and observe the buffaloes. Videotape the buffalo in its "almost" natural habitat. Play the video for your classmates.

A Step Beyond

1. Find and cut out pictures from magazines or newspapers of things the buffalo was used for. Draw a large picture of a buffalo. Glue each picture to the part of the buffalo that was used for the item.
2. Call or visit supermarkets or restaurants to ask if they sell buffalo meat. If so, encourage your mother to purchase some of the meat for sampling. Describe the taste.
3. Conduct a taste test to see if your classmates can distinguish between buffalo meat and regular beef.

Who Made What?

Tasks

1. Locate information on the following Native American inventions:
   - A. cigars
   - B. duck decoys
   - C. process for making chocolate
   - D. corn crib
   - E. process for making rubber
   - F. wheel
   - G. birch bark canoe
   - H. snowshoe
   - I. moccasins
   - J. toboggan
   - K. palisades
   - L. poncho
   - M. hammock
   - N. sign language
   - O. process for making rubber
   - P. bulbed syringe

A Step Beyond

1. Find out who invented the items in task one. Use the names and invention to create a flash card game.
2. Explain how each invention benefited the European settlers

Trail of Tears

Tasks

1. Use the General Index to the *World Almanac* to locate the pages on which the Trail of Tears is found.
2. Read the brief summary of the Trail of Tears. Take notes.
3. Explain how the Trail of Tears got its name.

A Step Beyond

1. Report on an incident in modern history which reminds you of the Trail of Tears.
2. Trace the route of the Trail of Tears on a road map of the United States. Use the legend to calculate the distance Native Americans were forced to travel.
3. Make a poster to show one fact that you learned about the Trail of Tears.

Statistically Speaking: Reservation Locations

Tasks

1. Use the General Index to the *World Alamnac* to find "Reservations".
   Locate your home state or a neighboring state if your state is not listed.
   - A. How many reservations are there in your state?
   - B. How many acres are owned by the tribe or tribes in your state?
   - C. How many acres are owned by individual Native Americans?
   - D. List the major tribe or tribes on the reservations in your state.

A Step Beyond

Construct a bar graph to show the number of reservations in the Midwest, Southwest, Southeast, and West. What do you think accounts for the large number of reservations in some regions and the small number in others?

Statistically Speaking: Landowners

Tasks

1. Use the latest world Almanac to find the three states with the largest number of Native American landowners (individually owned acreage).

   _____

   _____

   _____

2. Calculate the number of acres per Native American for
   California
   Colorado
   Kansas
   Florida

3. Calculate the average number of acres on each reservation (tribally owned acreage).
   Arizona
   Idaho
   Montana
   New Mexico
   Washington

A Step Beyond

Use a graphing software program to chart the data in task number 1.

Statistically Speaking: Wars and Battles

Tasks

Use the General Index to the *World Almanac* to answer the questions below:

1. List all of the entries that deal with <u>wars</u> or <u>battles</u>. Write the page number on which each is found.

   _____

   _____

   _____

   _____

   _____

2. Which three historical events occurred within six years of the "Trail of Tears"?

   _____

   _____

   _____

A Step Beyond

Compare the Tippecanoe Battle and the Battle of Wounded Knee. Write a short narrative explaining how life changed for Native Americans as a result of these two battles.

Historical Graffiti: El Morro

Tasks

1. Use the *Dictionary of American History* and other reference to find informationabout El Morro (Description Rock).
2. What does El Morro mean in Spanish? Where is El Morro located?
3. Who was the first explorer to leave an inscription on the rock?

A Step Beyond

1. Define GRAFFITI. Does the dictionary meaning differ from what you thought it was?
2. If you had been an explorer, what inscription would you have left on El Morro?
3. Invite students to paint or draw graffiti messages related to the history of El Morro.

What's In A Name?

Tasks

1. The Fitz Turner Commission for Human Relations and the Office of Anthropology, Smithsonian Institution compiled a list of names states that are of Native American origin. Study the list.

Origin of State Names

Prepared by the Fitz Turner Commission for Human Relations and Civil Rights, September, 1992 and the Office of Anthropology of the Smithsonian Institution.

ALABAMBA "Those who clear the land of thicket" (for farming purposes). The name of the Muskogean tribe, Alibamu. "Here we rest," Creek by origin.

ALASKA "Great County." Eskimo: al-ay-es-ka. A French interpretation of a Sioux word and a form of the word Kansas.

ARIZONA "Little Springs" or "few Springs." Papago: Ari-sonac or "Dry belt." Spanish: Aridda zona (Questionable)

ARKANSAS "Downstream People." French corruption of Algonquian name for the Quapaw.

CONNECTICUT "River of Pines." Algonquian name for the river Connittecock or Quonecktacut. Also means: "Long River," River Whose Water is Driven by Winds or Tides." Mohican, from the word Kw-Enht-Ekot, meaning "long river place."

DAKOTA (NORTH AND SOUTH) "Allies" or "Friends." Tribal name of the Sioux.

HAWAII Hawaiian, from the older form of the word Kawayi which meant "homeland."

IDAHO "IT IS SUN UP" OR "Behold the sun coming down the mountain." Also translated "Gen of the mountains." Shoshoni: contraction of exclamation: "Ee-da-how." Shoshone, named for an Indian tribe; Ida which means "salmon" and ho which means "eaters."

ILLINOIS "The men, perfect and accomplished." Name of an Algonquian tribe, Inini. Pronounced Illini by the French, meaning "man or warrior."

INDIANA "Land of the Indians." American language.

IOWA "Sleepy ones." Sioux: Alaouez. (Origin uncertain) Other meanings: "This is the place." "Beautiful land." Sioux, Ayuxawa, meaning "one who puts to sleep."

KANSAS "Wind people." "Small wind people of the south wind," or "Makes a breeze near the ground." Comes from the Wyandot Iroquois word for Plain. Sioux: Kansa. Also a tribal name.

KENTUCKY "Meadow land." Iroquois: Kentake. May also be: "Land of Tomorrow," Wyandot: Ken-ta-teh; "Drank and bloody ground." "River of blood." Ken-tuck-e; "Prairie," Cherokee.

MASSACHUSETTS "At or about the great hill." Algonquian, named for Massachusetts Indians, meaning "large hill place.

MICHIGAN "Great Water." Illinois Confederacy tribal name: Michigamea (Algonquian). Chippewa, probably from the word majiigan that means "clearing."

MINNESOTA "Whitish or sky-tinted water," "Clouded or turbid water," or "clear water." Kakota: Mine (water) and Sota (a description of the sky on certain days).

MISSISSIPPI Chippewa or Choctaw, meaning "large river."

MISSOURI "Muddy water." Incorrect meaning. Name of a tribe living at the mouth of the river. Algonquian: "canoe haver."

NEBRASKA Omaha, meaning "broad water."

NEW MEXICO "Land of Mexitli." Aztec: Mexitli, name of a god. Also named for the Aztec word for gold. The final syllable "co" comes from Sanskrit-ku "land."

OHIO "Great, fine, or beautiful river." Irouqois.

OKLAHOMA Term created in 1866 designating land held by the Choctaw. Choctaw: Two words meaning red people.

OREGON Disputed origin. "Plat or bark dish." Algonquian (Cree or Ojibwa). "Big-eared," Spanish: oregones; "Place of Plenty," Shoshone-Oyer-un-gen; "Beautiful Water,"

TENNESSEE Cherokee name for the ancient capital and then the river. Tanansi or Tennase.

TEXAS "Allies," "Friends," name applied to a group of tribes, Teyas. Also comes from the Spanish adaption of Caddo word teysha, meaning "hello, friend."

UTAH "In the tops of the mountains," tribal name of the Utes (Eutaw) who lived "high up" in the mountains. Apache, from Yuttahih meaning "one who is higer up."

WISCONSIN Chippewa, from miskonsin meaning "grassy place." Meaning unknown.

WYOMING "Upon the Great Plain," "The large meadows." Delaware, meaning "large prairie place." Popularized in 1809 by poet Thomas Cambell's tale of Gertrude of Wyoming.

Note: There are several spellings of ALGONQUIAN: Algonkian, Algonkin or Algonquin.

---

2. Complete the crossword puzzle using the states names in the list.

Across
1. red people
5. large hill place
6. here we rest
7. one who puts to sleep
8. one that is higher up
10. homeland
13. clearing
14. friend
16. milky or clouded water
19. large river

Down
2. plain or land
3. from the Aztec meaning "gold"
4. man or warrior
9. unknown
11. French interpretation of Kansas
12. Salmon eaters
15. canoe haver
17. hello, friend
18. beautiful

Word list: what's in a name?

Alabama
Alaska
Hawaii

Idaho
Illinois
Iowa
Kansas
Massachussets
Michigan

Minnesota
Mississippi
Missouri
New Mexico
North Dakota
Ohio

Oklahoma
Tennessee
Texas
Utah

From: Mateo, Ann. *Portraits of Native Americans,* 1992

3. Locate interesting places such as historical landmarks, cities, towns, land forms, and other geographic locations in your state that bear Native American names.

A Step Beyond

1. Research the tribes which settled in the places identified in task number three. What were the geographical or historical aspects which made the naming of each state appropriate? Use write-on transparencies to share your research.
2. Design and distribute a travel brochure, highlighting the places you've chosen to research.
3. Write to the tourist information centers of five states that have Native American names. Request information about the states. Read the information to see if there is any mention of its name originating with Native Americans. If this information is not included, write a letter recommending that it be included in future publications.

How Things Began

Tasks

1. Use the on-line search station or the card catalog to locate the following books which attempt to explain the origin of things:
    - A. *Earthmaker Tales*
    - B. *Teepee Tales Of The American Indians*
    - C. *Keepers Of The Earth*
2. Read the books listed in task number one and describe what phenomena the Native Americans are attempting to explain.

Beliefs and Superstitions

Tasks

1. What supernatural powers guided Native Americans through life?
2. Explain your understanding of the "Great Spirit".
3. Compare the "Great Spirit" to the "Guardian Angel".

A Step Beyond

Native Americans believe that they went to a Happy Hunting Ground when they died. Assume that you have a direct telephone line to the Happy Hunting Ground and you have a friend there. Call your friend to see how things are going. Write a dialog for your conversation. Record the conversation on an audiocassette player and share it with the class.

Medicine Man

Tasks

1. What is another name for the Native American medicine man? What special talents, powers, or training did the medicine man need?
2. Why was the medicine man a religious leader or helper?
3. What illnesses or diseases were Native Americans proned to have? What cures or remedies did the medicine men have for treating them?

A Step Beyond

Compare the two Native American curing societies, Mediwin Society of the Algonquins and False Face Society of the Iroquois.

Rituals and Ceremonies

Tasks

1. Use the on-line search station or the card catalog to find books or software about Native Americans.
2. Use the index or table of contents of the books to find information about Native Americans customs, rituals, or ceremonies.
3. Compare and contrast the marriage ceremony of at least two different tribes of your choice. Share your findings with the class.
4. Compare any one of the Native American marriage ceremonies to the marriage ceremony of your culture. Write a description of your comparison on a word processing program. Print your paper and share it with the class.

A Step Beyond

1. Use features of the marriage customs of various tribes to create your own marriage ceremony.
2. Perform a mock Native American marriage ceremony.

Bearing Gifts: Potlatch

Tasks

1. Search an encyclopedia on the CD ROM to find information about a "potlatch". Describe the potlatch ceremony of the Pacific coast Native American tribes.
2. What kinds of gifts were given at potlatches?
3. You want to give your Native American guest a special gift for potlatch. What would you give him and why?

A Step Beyond

Find other occasions where gifts are given in Native American cultures. Find occasions where gifts are given in your culture. How are they similar?

Sacred Animals

Tasks

1. Use the dictionary on the CD ROM to find the meaning of "sacred". Why were buffaloes considered to be sacred by the Native Americans?
2. According to the Native Americans, where did the buffalo originate?
3. Find out other groups of people who consider animals to be sacred. What are these animals?
4. Compare one of the animals you found in task number 3 to the buffalo. Which of the two animals do you consider to be most useful? Why?

A Step Beyond

1. Think about something or someone who is sacred to you. Demonstrate your feelings for the person or thing by introducing a declaration for a special festival day. Name the day and suggest proposed activities.
2. Compose a legend or tale about the buffalo spirit. Type the legend or tale on the computer. Illustrate and share with your class.

Traveling On!

Tasks

1. Native Americans introduced Europeans to objects such as the snow-shoe, toboggan, kayak, canoe, and moccasin. What do these items have in common?
2. With which tribe did each item in task number one originate? How do you think geography and climate influenced the invention of these objects?
3. Use the picture tour on CD ROM to find a picture and description of each item in task number one.

A Step Beyond

1. Use the READERS' GUIDE, INFOTRAC or another magazine index on CD ROM to locate articles about tobogganing, kayaking, and canoeing. Using illustrations, photographs, diagrams, and live action, if available, prepare a "How To" video on each sport.
2. Build a model of each item for a display of Native American inventions.

Music

Tasks

1. Use the dictionary on CD ROM to find the meaning of "maraca".
2. Using an on-line search station or the card catalog, find a book about musical instruments. Which instrument of the orchestra is similar to the maraca?
3. Which Native American tribe was noted for their music?
4. Collect, label and display items that the Native Americans used to make musical instruments.

A Step Beyond

1. Get a dried gourd from a grocery store. Use the gourd to make a musical instrument like the ones used by the Native Americans.
2. Find a recording of Native American music in your library.
3. Listen to the recording and try to recognize the instrument that you read about in task number two.
4. Choose one of the musical selections from the recording and create a dance for it. Demonstrate your dance for the class.

Games

Tasks

1. Use the on-line search station to find several Native American games. How important were games to the Native Americans?
2. What were some of the common items used to create their games? What were some of the prizes given?

A Step Beyond

1. Try playing some of the Native American games with members of the class. Each player will evaluate one of the games according to the check list below.

How Did They Rate?

1. Evaluate the game by circling a number from 1-5, 1 being the <u>lowest</u> and 5 being the <u>highest.</u>

Name of Game_____

Circle the Number

1. The game is easy easy to play.	1 2 3 4 5
2. The directions for playing the game are clear.	1 2 3 4 5
3. The game is fun.	1 2 3 4 5
4. The reward for winning is worth while.	1 2 3 4 5
5. The game time limit is adequate.	1 2 3 4 5
6. The game allows for a number of players.	1 2 3 4 5
7. The game allows a fair chance of winning.	1 2 3 4 5
8. I would like to play this game again.	1 2 3 4 5

2. Add the numbers you circled, and use the <u>rating scale</u> to determine how well the game you evaluated rated.

Rating Scale

1-8	Very Poor
9-14	Poor

---

2. Create a game based on the features you liked about the Native American game and teach it to the class.
3. Think of games that are played today. Which ones are similar to the Native American games?

Messages: Methods of Communicating

Tasks

1. Locate in books or other sources, five ways in which the early Native Americans communicated. Tell how and why each form of communication was used.
2. Bring to class an example of each form of communication for a classroom display. 3. Find the Cherokee number words and practice using them to count. Invite several of your classmates to practice counting with you.

A Step Beyond

1. What form of communication solved the communication problem among the many tribes of the Plains?
2. Learn to sign the message, I HAVE COME IN PEACE in Native American sign language. Teach it to your classmates.

Putting On An Act: The Song of Hiawatha

Tasks

1. Locate the play, "The Song of Hiawatha" in the *Play Index*. Find the anthology (book) in which the play is found and read it.
2. Locate the poem, "Hiawatha" by Longfellow in the *Index to Poetry for Children and Young People*. Read it.
3. In class, discuss the piay and the poem, paying special attention to each author's purpose.
4. Write your own version of the "Song of Hiawatha" for the stage.

A Step Beyond

1. Contact the manager of a local theater. Arrange to interview him or her.
2. Use the information gathered from the interview to prepare a cost estimate for producing the play you have written.

Putting On An Act: Plays About Native Americans

Tasks

1. Use the sample entry of the *Play Index* to answer the following questions:

   A. How many plays are listed under the topic, "Indians of North America?"

   B. List the titles of plays about people.

   _____

   _____

   _____

   _____

   _____

   _____

   C. Who wrote the play, "Jim Thorpe, All American?" _____

   D. Write a summary of the play.

A Step Beyond

1. Locate the play, "Jim Thorpe, All American." Read it.
2. Write a play about a contemporary athlete that you admire.

A Story, A Story: About Native Americans

Tasks

Use the sample entry from the *Short Story Index, 1984-88* to answer the following questions.

1. M. H. Austin wrote three books about basket makers. List them.

   _____

   _____

   _____

2. List two plays that M. H. Austin wrote.

   _____

   _____

3. Read *"The Basket Woman: First Story."* Write a character sketch of one of the main characters. Give specific examples of the laments of a short story found in "Basket Woman."

A Step Beyond

Messenger wrote a protest short story, *"Give it Back To the Indians."* Keeping in mind the elements of a short story, choose a subject about which you'd like to protest. Write a short story about it.

Telling Stories

Tasks

1. Read Native American stories, legends, and folk tales. Choose one to tell.
2. When you feel comfortable with the story, record it on an audio cassette tape.
3. Choose six of your classmates to join you in learning a story.

A Step Beyond

1. The seven STORYTELLERS, including yourself, will organize a storytelling festival. The seven of you will be the featured tellers at the festival.
2. Invite a local Native American storyteller to the Festival to tell stories. He or she will be the headliner storyteller.
3. Publicize the event in school and in the local news media.

Knots On A Counting Rope By Bill Martin

Tasks

1. Read the story, *Knots On A Counting Rope*, By Bill Martin.
2. Explain the purpose of a counting rope.
3. Describe the characters in the story. Where is the setting?
4. Why was the boy so named?
5. A metaphor makes an implied comparison between two different things—for example, "The sea of life;" a simile compares two different things using "as" or "like".
6. Re-read *Knots On A Counting Rope*. Make a list of as many metaphors and similes as you can recognize.
7. What effect did these figures of speech have on the story? Write your feelings on a computer writing program.

A Step Beyond

1. Visit an institution for the blind. Read a picture book to a blind child.
2. Ask the child to share with you what he sees in the story. Organize a touching/tasting/smelling game. Each time a person identifies an object, he/she ties a know in his rope. The person with the most knots wins the game.

Knots On A Counting Rope: What Is A Counting Rope

Tasks

1. Think of a time when you and your grandfather or another older person shared a very special time. Describe that special time orally with the class.
2. Use the poetry index or the index to poetry books to find poems about grandfathers. Do any of the descriptions fit your grandfather? If not, rewrite the poem to fit your grandfather.
3. The rope had a special purpose. What was it?
4. Bring items to class which are used to keep track of time. Explain to the class how each item is used to keep time.

A Step Beyond

1. Spend 15 minutes a day outside for a week blindfolded. Keep a journal of everything you experienced. Using a word processing program, write an essay indicating which of your senses were heightened during your experience.

Arts and Crafts

Tasks

1. Find out what animals were used by Native Americans to make or decorate various items. What parts of the animals were used and for what purpose?
2. What plants were used for making or decorating items?
3. In your opinion, which animal was most useful for making and decorating items?
4. Visit the Native American art section of a museum. Observe the motiff or symbols closely. Read the information accompanying the items on exhibit. Share this experience with the class.

A Step Beyond

1. Construct a bulletin board showing the parts of the animals used and the object made from it.
2. Invite the art teacher to bring examples of Native American art to class and talk about it.

Weavers

Tasks

1. From whom did the Navajo learn the art of weaving?
2. What was the first materials used by the Navajo for weaving?
3. Locate information in a variety of sources about Navajo weaving techniques.
4. Define the following words:
   - A. loom
   - B. warp
   - C. weft
   - D. weave
4. Draw a picture of a Navajo loom and label the parts.
5. Make a list of materials needed for making a Navajo rug.

A Step Beyond

1. Collect materials needed to make a box loom — shoe box top, pencil, ruler, string, yarn of various colors and scissors. Make several looms and place them, along with the yarn, in a learning center in the library or in your classroom.
2. Record on an audio cassette tape, step-by-step directions for weaving on a "box loom". Invite your classmates to weave on the looms.

Pottery

Tasks

1. What material was used for making pottery? Where was the material found?
2. What were some of the uses of pottery?
3. What different methods were used for making pottery?
4. View a videocassette or a filmstrip about Native American pottery making. Take notes for a discussion of your findings.

A Step Beyond

1. Ask the art teacher to demonstrate to the class how pottery is made.
2. Set up a display of the pottery made by the class. Invite other classes to view the display.

Basketmaking

Tasks

1. Use the dictionary on the CD ROM to define "dexterity". Think of activities where "dexterity" would be important. Demonstrate practical examples of "dexterity".
2. Explain the uses of the different kinds and sizes of Native American baskets.
3. Find samples of natural material that were used for basketmaking. Display the materials in the classroom.
4. Use the CD ROM and read about Native Americans basketmaking.
5. Who had the responsibility of making baskets?

A Step Beyond

1. Dye for basket fibers was made by boiling plant roots, flowers and seeds. With the help of your science teacher, make dye using the same procedures of Native Americans. Test your dye by submerging a white handkerchief or cloth in it.
2. Basketmaking became women's work. Form a debate team FOR or AGAINST the traditional roles of Native American women.

Agencies and Organizations: Where Do I Go?

Tasks

1. Consult the *National Directory, United States Government*, and other sources to identify the agencies/organizations listed below. Make a chart to show who heads them, why they were formed, their functions, and where their headquarters are located.
   - A. National Congress of American Indians
   - B. Council of Energy Resources Tribes
   - C. Bureau of Indian Affairs
   - D. Indian Claims Commission
   - E. National Indian Youth Council
   - F. American Indian Movement
   - G. International Treaty Council
   - H. Native American Rights Fund
   - I. National Indian Council on Aging
   - J. National Indian Health Board
   - K. Native American Science Education Association
2. Make a list of acronyms for the list above.

A Step Beyond

Read current magazine articles and newspaper accounts of Native American problems today. Clip articles or write a synopsis of them. On the basis of the articles, write a letter of inquiry or indignation to the appropriate agency.

Ancient Monuments

Tasks

1. Choose the best dictionary definition of monument as it relates to Native Americans ruins.
2. Use a variety of sources to gather information about the monuments listed below. Record the location, the tribe(s) who inhabited the area, and their historical importance.

   Aztec Ruins National Monument

   Bandlelier National Monument

   Canyon De Chelly National Monument

   Casa Grande National Monument

   Chaco Canyon National Monument

   Effigy Mounds National Monument

   Gila Cliff Dwellings National Monument

   Hovenweep National Monument

   Mesa Verde National Park

   Montezuma Castle National Monument

   Navajo National Monument

   Petrified Forest National Monument

   Walnut Canyon National Monument

   Wupatki National Monument
3. In which states are most of the monuments located?

A Step Beyond

1. Prepare a slide-tape show of the ancient monuments listed in task number two.
2. Go to a AAA office near you and request a road map of the Arizona, Colorado, New Mexico, and Utah area. Map out a route and an itinerary for a tour of monuments in these four states.

PART IV

Alaska

A Matter Of Statistics

Tasks

The Almanac has two indexes. QUICK REFERENCE in the back of the almanac, and the GENERAL INDEX in the front. The GENERAL INDEX lists specific topics in alphabetical order. Every important item is listed here, sometimes in more than one place.

1. Use the almanacs provided to answer the following questions:
    A. What is the highest point (elevation) in Alaska?
    B. What is the lowest point (elevation) in Alaska?
    C. When did the Gold Rush begin?
    D. What is the origin of Alaska's name?
    E. List the time zones in Alaska.
2. Collect statistics on the birth and death rates, marriages, divorces, income, and population of Alaskans.

A Step Beyond

1. Construct color graphs or use graphing software to compare birth and death rates, marriages, divorce income, and population of Alaskans for the past five years.
2. Display your graphs in your classroom. Explain the trends (decreases, increases) and describe what factors might have influenced the changes.

Icy Wilderness: The Purchase Of Alaska

Tasks

1. How much do you know about our 49th state?
   - A. When did Alaska become a state?
   - B. From what country was Alaska purchased?
   - C. When was it purchased?
   - D. How much did the United States pay for it?
   - E. Who was president at the time Alaska achieved statehood?
   - F. What other large land area did the United States purchase?
   - G. From whom was it purchased?
   - H. How much was paid for this land?
2. Do you consider Alaska a good buy for the money? Why or why not?

A Step Beyond

1. In terms of location, why was the purchase of Alaska a good idea?
2. What was William Seward's involvement with the purchase of Alaska? Why do you think so few people agreed with him?
3. Trace Alaska's history from purchase to statehood.
4. Organize a class debate FOR or AGAINST the purchase of Alaska.

Tall History: Totem Poles

Tasks

1. Use the glossary in any of the books about Alaska, Eskimos, or Native Americans to find a good definition of a totem pole.
2. Which cultural groups are most famous for their totem poles? What type of wood was used to carve totem poles? What subjects were most often carved on totem poles? For what occasions were they built?
3. What are storytelling totem poles? How are they read?

A Step Beyond

1. Ask your art teacher to assist you in carving a totem pole to tell something about your family or an Alaskan folk tale.
2. Make miniature totem poles out of paper towel rolls. Paint your stories on them, and make a totem pole village.

Alaska In The News: Exxon Valdez Oil Spill

Tasks

1. Study newspaper headlines of several newspapers.
2. Use the **Newsbank** or another newspaper index to find the latest account of the Exxon Valdez oil spill.
3. Write the name of the newspaper and the city of its publication.
4. Read the article about the oil spill and share it orally with the class.

A Step Beyond

Use the *Reader's Guide To Periodical Literature* to find a magazine article about Captain Joseph Hazelwood. Complete a magazine request form for the magazine or microfiche of the article. After reading the article, write a paragraph expressing whether you think Captain Hazelwood was negligent in the oil spill incident. If you think he was negligent, write a second paragraph stating what you would have done if you had been commanding the ship.

Alaska In The News: Alaskan Firsts

Tasks

1. Use the CD ROM or books about Alaska to complete the activity. What five events in Alaska's history would you consider to be headliners?
2. Summarize the five events and tell why you feel they would be headliners.
3. Consult many sources to find answers to these newsworthy "firsts".
   - A. Who was the <u>first</u> European to come to Alaska?
   - B. When was gold <u>first</u> discovered in Alaska?
   - C. When did Alaska's <u>first</u> newspaper begin publication?
   - D. What was the name of Alaska's <u>first</u> newspaper?
   - E. Who was Alaska's <u>first</u> delegate to the United States Congress?
   - F. When did Alaska's <u>first</u> territorial legislature convene?
   - G. When did Alaska hold its <u>first</u> election to choose state officials and United States Senators and Representatives?
   - H. When did Alaska's Marine Highway <u>first</u> begin operation?
   - I. Who was the <u>first</u> woman to win the Iditarod race?
   - J. Who made the <u>first</u> successful winter climb of Mt. McKinley?
   - K. When were the <u>first</u> salmon canneries built in Alaska?

A Step Beyond

Fold five large sheets of paper to resemble a newspaper. Write a newspaper headline for each of the headliners in task number one. Under each headline, write a lead paragraph.

Alaska In The News: Northern Exposure

Tasks

1. View an episode of NORTHERN EXPOSURE if it is aired on your local or cable television. Observe and take notes on the clothing, setting, climate, animals, and social life.
2. Is the program you viewed in task number 1 typical of what you have learned about Alaska? Why or why not? Give examples.

A Step Beyond

You have organized a sweepstakes guaranteeing the winners an all expense trip paid for two to Alaska. In advertising your sweepstakes, design a flyer and include the following information on it:

A. Title of sweepstakes
B. Registration procedures
C. Destination in Alaska
D. Date of trip
E. Value of trip
F. Mode of transportation
G. Name of hotel
H. Places of interest
I. Date winners will be announced

Distribute your flyers to classmates and encourage them to register for the trip to Alaska.

Gold Fever

Tasks

1. When was gold discovered in Alaska?
2. When did the Alaskan Gold Rush begin?
3. Choose the best dictionary definition of "prospector".
4. What is your interpretation of the phrase, "gold fever". Give an example of the meaning you found when reading about the Alaskan Gold Rush.
5. Other than climate, what special challenges or difficulties did the gold miners face in Alaska? (Consider where the gold deposits were found.)

A Step Beyond

1. Compare and contrast the Alaska and California Gold Rushes. What economic, cultural, social, and political effects did each have on the people?
2. Prepare a "before and after" chart of each Gold Rush to show your results.
3. If you were writing an advice column for the newspaper in the winter of 1900, what advice would you give potential prospectors before they left for Alaska?
4. Think of the discovery of something in your lifetime which has had a positive and a negative effect on society. Explain.
5. View a video tape which shows life during the Alaskan Gold Rush. Take note of the setting, the people, and the tools used for mining. Build a model of a 1900 gold mining town.

Land of The Midnight Sun

Tasks

1. Use the book, *Facts About the States* or any other book about states to answer the questions below.
   - A. What does "Alaska" mean?
   - B. Alaska has four nicknames. It is known as The Land of Midnight Sun, America's Last Frontier, Seward's Folly and Seward's Ice Box. Explain why each nickname was given.
   - C. Look carefully at the state seal of Alaska, taking note of all of the symbols.
2. Why do you think states have seals? Locate the seal for your state and several other states in your region. Look at the symbols on each seal. Do the symbols relate to the states' mottoes or name? Explain.

A Step Beyond

1. What is the one symbol on the seal of Alaska that could <u>not</u> appear on any other state seal? Explain the phenomenon.
2. Considering the geography, natural resources, and transportation of Alaska, do you think the designer/creator of the seal of Alaska did a good job? What would you add to the seal if you were designing it?
3. Make two 3 dimensional seals of Alaska, one to represent the seal currently in use and the other to represent your creation.

Where In Alaska?: Regional Differences

Each of Alaska's regions is distinctive. The regions are the southeast, south-central, south west, interior, far west, and arctic.

Tasks

1. Use atlases, books, magazine articles, the CD ROM, and filmstrips to gather information about the "specialness" of each region.
2. Of all the regions, which would you prefer to live in? Why?
3. Which region can best be described as the last frontier? Why?

A Step Beyond

1. Pretend you own an employment agency that specializes in placing workers in Alaska. Place people in the best region according to their occupational or professional experience or preference.
   - A. oil rig worker
   - B. pilot
   - C. lumberman
   - D. farmer
   - E. fisherman
   - F. totem pole artist
   - G. priest
   - H. hunter
   - I. ship captain
   - J. miner
   - K. dog musher
   - L. factory worker
2. Use the *Occupational Outlook Handbook* to locate the job description for all of the occupations in A Step Beyond number one. Use word processing software to write a want ad for the newspaper for three of the occupations listed.

Mapping It: Geography

An atlas contains maps and other geographical information.

Tasks

1. Look in any atlas index to find these places in Alaska. Write the page number and the coordinates for each, if given.
   - A. Alaska Highway _____
   - B. Aleutian Islands _____
   - C. Anchorage _____
   - D. Bering Sea _____
   - E. Kodiak Island _____
   - F. Big Lake _____
   - G. Mt. McKinley _____
2. Use the page numbers and coordinates to find the places in task number 1 in the atlas.

A Step Beyond

1. Draw a large political map of Alaska and make a legend for it to designate cities or towns, highways, islands, mountains, oceans or seas, and lakes. Put the places listed in task #l in their proper places on the map.
2. Make a relief map of Alaska to show the location of the major land forms. Include mountains, islands, lakes, seas, oceans, rivers, peninsulas, glaciers, and straits.

Boundaries

Tasks

1. Locate a map of Alaska on CD ROM or in an atlas. Study its boundaries carefully.
2. Draw a map of Alaska and label its boundaries on the north, south, east, and west.
3. Study a globe to see what countries are closest (geographically) to Alaska. In what ways have these countries influenced Native Alaska cultures?

A Step Beyond

Plan a cultural exchange program between Aleut, Eskimo, and Tlingit teens and Russian, Canadian, and Japanese teens. Each teen will live in the home of his or her host for six months. Prepare a guide for the exchange students, outlining the proper etiquette for visiting each culture.

Climate

Tasks

1. Use the dictionary on the CD ROM or a science dictionary to find the meaning of the words below.
    A. climate
    B. glacier
    C. ice age
    D. precipitation
    E. permafrost
2. Explain why some vegetables grow to be giant size in Matanuska.
3. Use an atlas to locate Barrow on the map. What is its location in relation to the "lower 48"?

A Step Beyond

Find still pictures or photographs of the words below. Use the visual maker to make slides of the pictures. Record information about each slide on an audio cassette. Present your slide show to the class.
A. aurora boralis
B. caribou
C. for-get-me-not
D. forest
E. igloo
F. lichens
G. parka
H. salmon
I. tundra
J. volcano

Cultures: Regional Customs And People

Tasks

1. Write a paragraph about the distinctive features of each of the cultures below.
   - A. Inupiat
   - B. Athabascan
   - C. Yupik
   - D. Koniag
   - E. Aleut
   - F. Tlingit

2. Place each cultural group in its proper geographical region on a map of Alaska. Use small pictures, different color push pins or flags to identify each cultural group.

3. According to the 1980 census, what is the population of each of the cultural groups in task number one? Construct a picture graph to show the distribution of the populations.

A Step Beyond

1. In your opinion, and based on your research, what do you think may have attributed to the decrease or increase in the populations of each ethnic culture?

2. For the group and region which experienced the greatest decline, prepare a sales pitch to entice people to move to that region. The pitch can be video, brochure, pamphlet, newspaper, magazine ads or a feature story.

Who Was Who?: Contributors To Alaskan History

Tasks

Match the person with his or her contribution to Alaska's history.

A. Victor Bering
B. William Seward
C. Joe Juneau
D. Dick Harris
E. John Muir
F. Benny Benson
G. Elizabeth Wanamaker Peratrovich
H. Marie Drake

1. Designed the state flag at the age of 12
2. President of the Alaska Native Sisterhood
3. Danish explorer who discovered a strait
4. Discovered gold and started the gold rush
5. Wrote the state song
6. Secretary of State, persuaded the United States to purchase Alaska
7. Discovered gold and started the gold rush
8. Naturalist

A Step Beyond

Pretend you are a reporter for the **ALASKAN STAR MAGAZINE.** Write a "profile" story about John Juneau, Marie Drake, Elizabeth Wanamaker Peratrovich and William Seward.

Home Sweet Home: Types Of Housing

Tasks

Shelter is as important to the Eskimo as food.

1. Find examples of Eskimo and Aleut housing on CD ROM, filmstrips, and videocassettes. Write your description of each type of home.
2. List the building materials needed to construct an igloo and a sod house.
3. Which house is the most economical to build? Which house can be built in less time?
4. How has housing for Eskimos and Aleutians changed in the last decade?

A Step Beyond

1. Draw the floor plan of a traditional igloo and sod house. Explain the significance of the arrangement of the rooms or areas.
2. Use sugar cubes to build a model of an igloo.
3. Use popsicle sticks and clay to build a model of a sod house.

Dressing Up: Regional Clothing

Tasks

1. Locate in various sources, a description of the following clothing worn by Alaskans.
    - A. hunters' clothing
    - B. kuspuk
    - C. mukluks
    - D. parka
    - E. underwear
    - F. women's clothing
    - G. mittens
2. How has modern technology changed the way Alaskans dress? Give some examples.
3. Write a report on one piece of clothing listed in task number I.

A Step Beyond

1. Pretend you are a world famous designer of Alaskan clothing. Sketch some designs of clothing for men and women for your summer and winter line.
2. Gather as many of the furs, fabrics, and other materials as you can for a display to go with your sketches.
3. Contact a local furrier to request samples of the types of furs used for the construction of Alaskan clothing. Ask the furrier to explain the special qualities of each fur.

Reservations

Tasks

1. Explain what a reservation is, and why reservations were established.
2. Write the <u>best</u> definition of reservation as it relates to Native American or Alaska Natives' land.
3. Find in an almanac the number of acres owned by tribes or tribal nations in Alaska. Compute the average number of acres per person.
4. How does the number of acres per person compare with Native American land ownership in Montana, Oklahoma, and Washington?

A Step Beyond

1. On a map of Alaska, locate the Native American Indian tribes. Is there a particular area "reserved" for them as is done in the "lower 48"? Explain your answer.
2. Hold a summit meeting with the Native Americans of Montana, Oklahoma, Washington, and Alaska meeting to discuss land issues.

Fact or Fiction

Tasks

1. Read the statements below about Alaska. If you believe a statement is factual, write "yes" at the end. If you think a statement is fiction, write "no" at the end. Defend your answer with information from the CD ROM or other reference sources.

    A. All Eskimos in Alaska live in igloos.

    B. The only mode of transportation in Alaska is the sled pulled by sled dog teams.

    C. Eskimo parents are strict and they spank their children frequently.

    D. Eskimo children never go to bed because it never gets dark.

    E. Eskimo children are not very happy because it is always too cold to play outside.

2. Use the on-line search station or the card catalog to find one fiction book about Alaska and one nonfiction book about Alaska.
3. Read the books you found in task #2.
4. Compare the two books. Be able to tell the class why each book is classified as it is.

A Step Beyond

You moved to the most northern part of Alaska, next door to a mysterious, busy little man who is sometimes seen in a red suit. Be a detective and gather the facts about this man. Write a biography about the little man to be released in December. Have a book signing session.

Works of Art

Tasks

1. Find examples of Native Alaskan masks, totem poles, chilkat blankets, jewelry, baskets, canoes, wood or ivory carvings, and pottery in books, magazines, on laser discs, and CD ROM.
2. Define art. How do the art objects in task number 1 fit the definition of art?
3. Although most of the art forms in task number 1 serve useful purposes, they are considered art. Draw three columns on a sheet of paper. Label the columns ornamental, ceremonial, or utilitarian. Classify the art objects from task # 1 under the appropriate columns on your sheet.

A Step Beyond

Visit a local museum to view the different art objects similar to those listed in task number one. Write all evidences of Native American influence you observe in the objects.

Transportation: Motorized

Tasks

1. Use an encyclopedia on CD ROM or an almanac to compare the number one mode of transportation in Alaska to the number one mode of transportation in the lower 48. Why is each essential to the citizens?
2. In Alaska the small airplane is as important as the family car in the lower 48. What other means of transportation are crucial to Alaskans? Under what circumstances are they used?

A Step Beyond

1. If there is a ferry in your area, contact the company that operates it to request an educational tour.
2. Plan a field trip aboard the ferry.
3. Develop questions relative to the history, the operations, and uses of a ferry to be used as discussion questions for a field trip.
4. Take a camcorder and record the trip.

Transportation: Sled Dogs

Tasks

1. What people and what areas in Alaska still make use of sled dogs? Give reasons for their continued use.
2. What modern method of transportation is gradually replacing the sled dogs?

A Step Beyond

1. Make a model of the two most important modes of transportation in Alaska. Display your models in the classroom.
2. Which mode of transportation would you use for the situations below? Choose from airplane, automobile, sled dog, ferry, snowmobile, train, or patrol boat.
   A. You need to deliver medical supplies to a small remote village in Barrow.
   B. You want to travel from Cordova to Kodiak and you do not want to leave your car behind.
   C. You live in Sitka, but have to attend a business meeting in Nome.
   D. You live in Atkasook and you are going to school at Meade River.
   E. You have planned a sightseeing trip from Fairbanks to Denali National Park.
   F. As a policeman, you are assigned to guard the area between Craig and Sitka.

Did You Know?: Facts

Tasks

1. Read the information on the encyclopedia on CD ROM. Each time you see information that is entirely new to you, write a "did you know" question about it. Write the answer to each of your "did you know" questions.
2. Cut out pictures from old magazines, brochures, and newspapers to make a collage of new information you learned about Alaska.

A Step Beyond

1. Use the "did you know" questions in task #1 to create a "War of the Brains" television game that you will organize and sponsor.
2. Create three, 30 seconds television commercials advertising Alaskan products. Air the commercials during the "War of the Brains".

In The Index

Tasks

1. An encyclopedia index guides you to specific volumes and pages in a set of encyclopedias. Use the index of *World Book Encyclopedia* to locate specific topics about Alaska. Write the volume and page number for each topic on the line beside it.
   - A. Alaska Time Zones _____
   - B. Alaska Native Brotherhood_____
   - C. Alaskan malamute_____
   - D. Alaska Panhandle _____

2. The following, "If I were..." questions can be answered using the sample index for task number 1.
   - A. If I were looking for a picture of a glacier, I would find it in volume_____, page_____.
   - B. If I were looking for information on land use issues of Alaskan Natives, I would find it in volume_____, page_____.
   - C. If I were interested in places to visit in Alaska, I would look in volume_____, page_____.
   - D. If I were looking for the major mountains in Alaska, I would find it in volume_____, page_____.
   - E. If I were doing a report on the Alaskan brown bear, I would find it in volume_____, page_____.

A Step Beyond

1. Prepare and present a lesson on how to use an encyclopedia index to locate general information about Alaska. Use visuals such as transparencies, video, filmstrips, and maps in your lesson.
2. Design an "index hunt", a puzzle or a game about Alaska.

State Motto

Tasks

1. Use the CD ROM or WORLD ALMANAC to find the motto of Alaska.
2. In your opinion, does the motto fit the state? Explain your answer.
3. Using a computer writing program, write a paragraph describing the meaning of Alaska's motto.
4. Look at the mottoes of other states. Do any of the mottoes indicate cardinal directions?

A Step Beyond

Create an imaginary 51st state. Give the state a name and think of a motto to go with it. Cite your reason for arriving at your particular motto and state name. Recommend your imaginary state to Congress for statehood.

By The Numbers

Tasks

The vastness of Alaska makes it a mathematician's dream. Calculate the following:

1. How much taller is Mt. McKinley, Alaska than Mt. Whitney, California?
2. Alaska's total area is 591,004 square miles. About a third of the area is forested. How many square miles is forested?
3. What percentage of Alaska is lakes and rivers if lakes and rivers comprise 19,980 square miles?
4. The Arctic Circle also makes up a third of the total area. How many square miles is it?
5. In 7 years, the population of Alaska rose from 401,851 to 525,000. What was the total increase?
6. Find the Eskimo numerals for 1-10. Put them on strips of poster board and post them in your classroom.

A Step Beyond

Gather statistical information from *Facts About The States, World Almanac*, and other sources to create word problems for an Alaska Math Bowl. Choose two teams of 3 students to complete. (Remember, you have to calculate the problems yourself first.)

Animals: Roaming The Land

Tasks

1. Use the CD ROM, a science or animal encyclopedia or other books about animals to get a description of the Alaskan animals below:
    A. black bear
    B. brown grizzly bear
    C. polar bear
    D. bison
    E. caribou
    F. moose
    G. musk ox
2. If you could train one, which of the animals listed in task number 1 would you want for a pet? Why?
3. Make a list of animals common to your community that you might see on any given day.

A Step Beyond

You are coming home from school and you see a moose in your yard. Write a humorous account of your reaction and feelings about this experience.

Animals: From The Water

Tasks

1. Fish, whales, dolphins, seals, walruses, and sea otters are plentiful in Alaska. Use the on-line search station to find information about the sea mammals listed above.
2. Use the READERS' GUIDE, INFOTRAC or other massive databases to locate articles on all of the sea mammals listed in task number one.
3. Draw, paint, or cut from an old magazine pictures of the sea mammals in task number one. Paste or tape the pictures on a large map of Alaska where they are found most abundantly.

A Step Beyond

Each of the sea mammals in task #1 provide food and other products for the Eskimos, Aleuts, and Indians of Alaska. Design a mobile of the whale, the seal and the walrus to show some of their uses, other than food.

Animals: Whales

Tasks

1. The whale has been useful to the Eskimos for many reasons. Use the CD ROM or encyclopedia to find out how the Eskimos used the following:
    - A. blubber
    - B. oil
    - C. baleen
    - D. bones
    - E. meat
2. The baleen whale has no teeth, but it does not starve. How did nature provide for its eating?

A Step Beyond

1. Use a book about the elements of poetry and read about jingles. Write a jingle about the use of whales. Example:
   Your meat is good to eat
   It is yummy
   And it fills my tummy.
2. Find pictures of different whales in encyclopedias or books about whales. Study the physical features of whales. If you do not think the name given is appropriate for a whale, rename it and give your reasons for doing so.

Animals: Salmon

Tasks

1. Why and what commercial name has been given to the city of Ketchikan?
2. Explain the amazing journey made by the salmon swimming against the current.
3. Find the names of different kinds of salmon. Write a description of each, using a computer program. Find or draw a picture of each kind of salmon for the information you found. Attach the printed information and the picture of the salmon on poster boards for display.

A Step Beyond

1. Use the information you found about the salmon to host an "Everything You Wanted to Know About the Salmon, But Never Had the Answer" session. Compose ten questions about the salmon. Write the answer to each question and give each to a different classmate. Students will be recognized by you to read the answer to their question. You will provide the question for each answer given. You may evaluate the session by asking the students if they learned something they didn't know before.
2. Ask your mother or another adult to help you prepare the recipe below.

Salmon Roll
1 can (16 ounces) red salmon
½ cup chopped pecans
1package (8 ounces) cream cheese, softened
3 tablespoons chopped fresh parsley
2 drops liquid smoke or Worchestershire sauce
crackers
Combine salmon, cream cheese and liquid smoke or Worchestershire; mix well. Shape into ball or log. Roll in mixture of pecans and parsley. Roll up in plastic or wax paper. Chill to blend flavors. Serve with crackers.

Animals: For The Birds

Tasks

1. Which species of birds are most abundant in Alaska?
2. What is Alaska's official bird?
3. What special characteristics do all of the birds have which enable them to adapt to the climate?
4. Describe the habitats of the Arctic tern, the puffin, and the loon. What other state or states would these three birds be able to survive in? Explain.

A Step Beyond

1. Draw and color or paint pictures of the birds you found in task number one. List four or five important or interesting facts about each bird.
2. Using easily found objects such as pieces of wood and moss, build a diorama of the habitat of one of the birds in task number one.

Booked Up: *America The Beautiful* By Ann Heinrich.

Tasks

Card catalogs that are on computers may be accessed from on-line search stations. You still look for books by author, title, and subject, but you are also able to search by using keywords. The following is a SUBJECT SEARCH. Our subject is ALASKA.

SUBJECT SEARCH

1. Since we know that the subject we're looking for is ALASKA, we highlight subject from the list of options (menu) at the bottom of the screen. PRESS ENTER

Search Plus   Press F1 for Help

Subject   Title   Author   Call Number   Series
Keyword

2. In the highlighted area, type ALASKA. PRESS RETURN

Search Plus   Press F1 for Help

Subject: ALASKA

3A. An alphabetical list of subjects will appear on the screen. This list will include ALASKA. Use the down arrow key to highlight ALASKA. PRESS ENTER

Search Plus   Subjects   Press F1 for Help

1	Airplanes—Piloting
1	Airplanes—Speed records
1	Airports
1	Airports—Employment
2	Airships
1	Akihito, Crown Prince, son of Hirohito, Emperor of Japan, 1933-
2	Alabama
1	Alabama—Fiction
4	Alaska
6	Alaska—Fiction
6	Alaska—History

When you choose ALASKA, a complete record for the book will appear on the screen. It will have the same information on it that a traditional card catalog card has. Author, title, publication information, annotation, subject headings, and call number. In addition, the on-line card catalog tells you if copies of a particular book are available. See record below.

3B

979.8
HEI

TITLE: Alaska
AUTHOR: Heinrichs, Ann
SERIES: America the Beautiful
PUBLISHED: Chicago: Childrens Press, 1991
MATERIAL: 144p. color photos.
NOTE: Discusses the land, people, history, government, economy, sports, and recreation of Alaska.

1. Use the sample record in task 3B to complete the following statements:
     A. The title of the book is _____.
     B. The complete call number for this book is _____.
     C. The book was published in _____.
     D. Copies are_____available.
     E. This book is about _____.
2. Would the book in task #3B be useful if you were doing a report on the history of Alaska?

A Step Beyond

1. Find other books about Alaska which deal with similar topics as the one in task number three B.
2. Make an annotated bibliography of the titles you would recommend to your classmates to use for their reports on Alaska.

In Other Words: Definitions of Alaskan Words

Tasks

1. Use a dictionary or the dictionary on CD ROM to define the following words:

   A. Alaska
   B. aurora borealis
   C. blubber
   D. bush
   E. cheechako
   F. glacier
   H. parka
   I. permafrost
   J. tundra

2. From the definitions, write short clues for each of the words in task number 1. Use crossword puzzle software to create a puzzle.

A Step Beyond

Construct a mobile to represent aurora borealis, parka, tundra, and glacier. Before hanging them, explain each word to the class.

Poetry: An Arctic Vision

Tasks

1. A number of places are mentioned in the poem, "An Arctic Vision". List them. Name a major city close to each place.
2. Locate the places in "An Arctic Vision" in an atlas and give the coordinates.
3. What animals are featured in the poem?

A Step Beyond

1. Read the poem, "An Arctic Vision" aloud to the class. Using a projection device such as an LCD or computer monitor, show your classmates where each place in the poem is located.
2. Prepare a slide tape show interpretation of the poem.

Point of View

Tasks

1. Use a poetry index to find the poems, "The Klondike", "An Arctic Vision", "Alaska", and the "Cremation of Sam Magee" in various poetry anthologies.
2. Make photocopies of the poems, write the poems on separate sheets of paper, or use word processing software to print them.
3. In each of the poems in task number 1, there is some kind of conflict.
    A. Identify the poem(s) which have conflict between man and nature.
    B. Identify poem(s) which have conflict between man and man.
    C. Identify the poem which shows conflict between man and himself.

A Step Beyond

Draw a cartoon strip of no more than 10 frames for each of the poems in task number 1.

A Story, A Story: Songs And Stories

Tasks

1. The stories and poems of a culture tell so much about the beliefs and superstitions of that culture. Read the stories and poems in *Eskimo Songs And Stories* and classify them according to "How and Why", "Fable", or "Superstition". The largest number of stories/poems fall into which category?

2. What is being described in the first story in *Eskimo Songs And Stories*? Read the poem on audio cassette and give your interpretation of it.

3. Think of a story that you remember your mother or grandmother telling you which you consider very important. Explain why this particular story is so important to you. Tell the story to your class.

A Step Beyond

1. Choose a "creation" story from *Eskimo Song And Stories*. Compare this story with a creation story from Virginia Hamilton's *In The Beginning.....* Write and produce a play based on the two creation stories.

A Story, A Story: *Julie Of The Wolves* By Jean C. George

Tasks

1. Read the book, *Julie Of The Wolves in class.*
2. In your opinion, what is the author's purpose for writing the story?
3. Does the description of the setting give you any clue as to what state this story takes place? Is a place named? If so, what is it? Locate the place on a map of the United States.
4. Read a nonfiction book about Alaska, copyrighted within the last five years. Based on the factual information you read, how accurate is the setting in *Julie Of The Wolves*?
5. View the video, *White Fang.* Compare the characters and setting to *Julie Of The Wolves.*

A Step Beyond

1. Design a series of bookmarks for National Library Week showing your favorite scenes in *Julie Of The Wolves.* Give each bookmark a simple caption.
2. Write a diary from Julie's perspective about her experiences with the wolves.
3. Write an additional chapter to *Julie Of The Wolves.*

Popular Pastime: Making String Figures

Tasks

1. What is a superstition?
2. Read the story, "Totanguak" in the book, *Eskimo Songs And Stories.* Identify the superstition.
3. What were the challenges made to the child? What were the rules? What was the consequence?
4. Does this story remind you of any other stories you've heard or read? If so, how?

A Step Beyond

1. Making string figures is a popular pastime among children of many cultures. Find information about forming string figures. On large poster boards, write and illustrate directions for forming them.
2. From the images in the story, try to visualize what a Spouting Whale and a Man Carrying Kayak look like. Create string figures of each.
3. Give a live demonstration for making string figures.

Games n' Things

Tasks

1. Eskimos found numerous ways to amuse themselves. Use the on-line search station to search for books about Alaskan/Eskimo/Indian games.
2. Locate the following games in the indexes of the books you found.
   - A. arm pull
   - B. ayagak
   - C. blanket toss
   - D. four man carry
   - E. greased pole walk
   - F. kneel jump
3. Give the directions for making the Eskimo toy, ayagak. Write the directions for playing with the ayagak and post them in your class.

A Step Beyond

1. Using available materials, make four ayagaks. Organize four teams to test their skills in playing the game.
2. Organize an Eskimo-Indian Olympics and ask your classmates to participate in the games or your adaptation of the games in task number 2.

A National Sport: Dog Sledding

Tasks

1. What are artifacts? How are they important to the game, "Dog Sled Ambassadors" ?
2. Play the MECC computer game, "Dog Sled Ambassadors". From the menu, choose the number of artifacts you will accept, a team of five dogs, your teammate, and equipment.
3. Draw a diagram of a dog-sled team. Tell what each dog does.
4. In what part of the state are the following places in the game located?
   A. Bering Sea
   B. Nome
   C. Seward Peninsula
   D. Yukan Delta

A Step Beyond

1. Construct a flow chart to show how the decisions you made in the beginning of the game affected the final outcome of the game, the number of problems you encountered, and the amount of time it took you to complete the game.
2. Construct a board game about "dog-sledding" which requires many of the same decisions as those in Dog Sled Ambassadors. Take the players into different parts of the state and have them interact with different cultures.

A National Sport: Iditarod

Tasks

1. Dog Mushing is Alaska's national sport. What is it?
2. What is the Iditarod Race? How did the race get its name? Trace the Iditarod Trail from Nome, Alaska to the finish line.
3. Write a letter to the Iditarod Trail Committee, Inc., P. O. Box 870800, Wasilla, AK 99687 to request a student information packet.

A Step Beyond

1. When the student information packet arrives, make a poster announcing the upcoming race.
2. Post the names of the mushers and their racing experience on the bulletin board.
3. Divide your class into four teams and have each team choose a musher for the Iditarod Race
4. Follow the race on a sports channel, in the newspaper, or write the Iditarod Trail Committee for the results of the race.

Index